Corporate Governance: Accountability in the Marketplace

Second edition

ELAINE STERNBERG

The Institute of Economic Affairs

Second edition published in Great Britain in 2004 by
The Institute of Economic Affairs
2 Lord North Street
Westminster
London SW1P 3LB
in association with Profile Books Ltd

First edition published in 1998 by
The Institute of Economic Affairs

The mission of the Institute of Economic Affairs is to improve public understanding of the fundamental institutions of a free society, with particular reference to the role of markets in solving economic and social problems.

A CIP catalogue record for this book is available from the British Library.

ISBN 0 255 36542 X

Many IEA publications are translated into languages other than English or are reprinted. Permission to translate or to reprint should be sought from the Director General at the address above.

Typeset in Stone by MacGuru Ltd
info@macguru.org.uk

Printed and bound in Great Britain by Hobbs the Printers

CONTENTS

THE AUTHOR

Elaine Sternberg is Principal of Analytical Solutions, a London consultancy firm specialising in business ethics and corporate governance (www.ethicalgovernance.com; es@ethicalgovernance. com). She is also a Research Fellow in Philosophy at the University of Leeds, where she has helped the Centre for Business and Professional Ethics develop an MA in Business Ethics and Corporate Governance. She worked for fourteen years as an investment banker in London, New York and Paris; while in the City, she founded and ran two multi-million pound profitable businesses for her employers. Previously, she was a Lecturer and Fulbright Fellow at the London School of Economics, where she earned her doctorate. A member of the Academic Advisory Council of Public Concern at Work, Dr Sternberg is the author of *Just Business: Business Ethics in Action* (second edition, Oxford University Press, 2000; first edition, Little, Brown, London, 1994; Warner paperback, 1995), *The Stakeholder Concept: A Mistaken Doctrine* (The Foundation for Business Responsibilities, 1999) and many articles on business ethics and corporate governance.

FOREWORD

Corporate governance has been under the microscope in recent years. The failures of Enron and WorldCom and the associated 'bursting' of what many investors regarded as a stock market bubble in the prices of Information and Communications Technology shares led many to question the regulation surrounding corporate governance. Other issues have also arisen that have given rise to debates about the regulation of corporations, for example, executive pay, the accountability of privatised utilities etc. Politicians have tried to satiate the demand for action by instituting reviews (for example, Hampel, Higgs etc.) and by legislation and regulation (for example, the US Sarbanes-Oxley Act). But the debate around these issues appears wholly confused.

The particular issues that have led to unease are often manifestations of the divorce between ownership and control that can arise as a result of private corporations being managed by executives. This is not necessarily an inevitable aspect of the corporate form of business organisation but that form of organisation certainly makes a partial separation, if not a divorce, between ownership and control possible. But, one is entitled to ask whether, if this is the problem, what business is it of government to try to solve it. It is shareholders who lose from excessive executive pay, from accounting scandals and so on. It is the responsibility of shareholders to deal with these problems. However, there seems to be a wider agenda amongst policymakers. As far as the electorate is concerned, demands for action may arise as a result of a perceived sense of injustice or unfairness in the outcomes of accounting scandals and executive pay decisions. However, academics, journalists and politicians are often calling for nothing less than a complete realignment of the way in which companies are regulated. Often this will involve calls for the German/Japanese model of regulation or perhaps the 'stakeholder model' of regulation to be implemented. In the latter, companies are apparently accountable to a wide range of diffuse interests. In reality, the difficulties of ensuring accountability to diffuse interests means that companies following that model are frequently captured by a self-serving management following its own objectives.

In the second edition of *Corporate Governance: Accountability in the Marketplace*, Dr Sternberg separates and analyses the relevant issues in a way fitting for a philosopher. She updates the first edition to take into account recent developments such as the Enron scandal and the associated regulatory response.

She begins by defining precisely the meaning of corporate governance. Corporate governance is the mechanism by which corporate actions, assets and agents are directed at achieving corporate objectives established by the corporation's shareholders. Thus common criticisms of corporate governance are frequently misdirected. They are, implicitly, criticisms of the corporate ends. Those who prefer the German/Japanese model or stakeholder models to the Anglo-American model of corporate governance would, in fact, prefer corporate efforts to be redirected away from satisfying the objectives of the owners of the corporation.

Dr Sternberg shows that these alternative models have profound implications for property rights and freedom of contract. If corporations that use the property of shareholders find that they have to be accountable to a range of different interests, the security of property is undermined fundamentally. Also, if the corporation is accountable to a range of groups whose legal interest cannot possibly be defined the corporation is, in reality, accountable to nobody. This is a licence for management to pursue its own objectives. The German/Japanese model of corporate governance in particular has demonstrably failed to produce a more efficient corporate sector, a less corrupt corporate sector or a healthier economy.

Dr Sternberg critiques the Anglo/American system and does find faults with it. These faults can be addressed by making the system work in practice how it is supposed to work in theory – we should not adopt alternative theories of governance. It is unlikely that the system can be improved considerably by further regulation. However, existing regulations do impair corporate governance and these could be repealed or replaced. Dr Sternberg suggests that there should be 'competition in the market place' for corporate governance mechanisms. Companies have to compete for investment funds and those with the best mechanisms for governing the corporation should find that shareholder value is increased and required returns on capital reduced. Different forms of corporate governance, audit procedures, information disclosure requirements and so on are appropriate for different forms of organisation. Ultimately it is the responsibility of the shareholders to ensure that the management use the assets of the company to fulfil corporate objectives. Regulatory restraints on the evolution of mechanisms of corporate governance should be removed.

Dr Sternberg's arguments deserve serious consideration. Policymakers seem to forget that the recent scandals in corporate governance have arisen at a time when companies are more heavily regulated than at any other time in the history of the limited liability corporation. Perhaps the experiment with prescriptive regulation has failed. Policymakers also seem to forget that the recent scandals did in fact relate to a failure of management and perhaps directors, in certain notable cases, to pursue the objectives of shareholders. It is legitimate to ask, whether this problem should not be solved by shareholders rather than by government. Dr Sternberg's updated second edition is timely indeed. It separates the issues very effectively and makes an important contribution to the debate: one that should be taken seriously by academics, journalists, commentators and politicians.

The views expressed in Hobart Paper 147 are, as in all IEA publications, those of the author and not those of the Institute (which has no corporate view), its managing trustees, Academic Advisory Council member or Senior staff.

PHILIP BOOTH

Editorial and Programme Director,
Institute of Economic Affairs.
Professor of Insurance and Risk Management,
Sir John Cass Business School, City University.
November 2003

ACKNOWLEDGEMENTS

I would like to thank Daniel Moylan and David Weisberg whose constructive criticisms of the text of the first edition did much to improve it.

E.S.

SUMMARY

- Contrary to popular opinion, businesses and corporations are not the same thing: not all corporations are businesses, and most businesses are not corporations. Whereas 'business' designates a particular objective, 'corporation' designates a particular organisational structure.
- Corporate governance refers to ways of ensuring that corporate actions, agents, and assets are directed at achieving the corporate objectives established by the corporation's shareholders (as set out in the corporation's Memorandum of Association or comparable constitutional document).
- Many criticisms of corporate governance are based on false assumptions about what constitutes ethical conduct by corporations, and confusions about what corporate governance is.
- Protests against takeovers, 'short-termism', redundancies and high executive remuneration are typically objections to specific corporate outcomes, not criticisms of corporate governance.
- Many misguided criticisms of the Anglo-American model come from confusing corporate governance with government: it is a mistake to criticise corporations for not achieving public policy objectives, and for not giving their stakeholders

the rights and privileges commonly associated with citizenship.

- Some criticisms of the traditional Anglo-American model of corporate governance are justified. There are serious practical obstacles that prevent shareholders from keeping their corporations and corporate agents properly accountable.
- Though commonly praised, the German and Japanese systems are considerably less capable of achieving the definitive purpose of corporate governance than the Anglo-American model. Neither is designed to protect, nor typically used for protecting, property rights.
- The increasingly popular stakeholder doctrine is also incapable of providing better corporate governance. The stakeholder doctrine is intrinsically incompatible with all substantive objectives, and undermines both private property and accountability.
- Regulation that attempts to improve corporate governance by limiting shareholders' options, and reducing their freedom to control their own companies as they choose, is necessarily counterproductive.
- The way to respond to flaws in current Anglo-American corporate governance mechanisms is to improve the accountability of corporations to their ultimate owners, preferably by having corporations compete for investment, and institutional investors for funds, in part on the degree of accountability they offer to their beneficial owners.

AUTHOR'S PREFACE TO THE SECOND EDITION

Since *Corporate Governance: Accountability in the Marketplace* was first published in 1998, corporate governance has attracted ever greater public attention. Even before the Enron and WorldCom scandals, the Cadbury and Greenbury reports had been followed by the Hampel, Turnbull, and Myners inquiries in Britain, and by countless official and other inquiries worldwide.

Post Enron, governance has become a favoured scapegoat, blamed for any number of major – often seriously misdiagnosed – ills. In the media frenzy, 'Enron' has been used to designate concerns as diverse as 'gatekeeper' failures, questionable auditor and board independence, rapid share price falls, financial innovation, high executive and directorial remuneration, opaque financial statements, the use of judicial powers to destroy suspects, loss of investor confidence, financial engineering, lack of analyst independence, wide diversification of company activities, multiple conflicts of interest, off-balance sheet financing, incomplete deregulation, limited pension fund diversification, the use of special purpose entities, faddish investing, ideological regulation, etc. etc..

Reflecting that long list, misguided commentators have denounced the Anglo-American system of corporate governance, claiming that it has lost whatever legitimacy it might once have had.[1] 'Enron' has been invoked as the justification for all sorts of ill-conceived governmental initiatives[2] – both in the United States and in jurisdictions far from it.

Those reactions are, however, seriously mistaken. Most of the matters for which 'Enron' has become shorthand have little or no relation to corporate governance properly understood. And what Enron did show about corporate governance, was that the Anglo-American system works. No system can prevent all the problems to which complex human arrangements are liable.[3] Systems are properly judged on their ability to reduce the frequency and severity of misdeeds, and by their ability to detect and correct the problems that do arise. By those standards, Enron is in fact evidence of the effectiveness and resilience of the Anglo-American system. Enron's wrongdoing was detected not by the regulators, but by the market. The misdeeds received swift and conclusive punishment from the market itself … long before the first government investigation was convened. And despite the many moral hazards generated by the regulatory framework, Enron and WorldCom remain exceptional cases of wrongdoing. As the serious scandals and major corporate[4] failures of Europe, Asia, Africa and Australia demonstrate, no system has worked better.

That is not to deny that Anglo-American corporate governance has been defective in some prominent cases. Some companies

1   Consider, for example, John Plender's assessment in *Going Off the Rails* (John Wiley, 2003; excerpted in 'Casting a shadow on capitalism', *Financial Times*, 28 January 2003, p. 14).

2   See Chapter 7 below.

3   As the (UK) Higgs Report on the *Review of the role and effectiveness of non-executive directors* correctly states, 'No system of governance can or should fully protect companies and investors from their own mistakes.'; Derek Higgs, The Department of Trade and Industry, January 2003, ('Higgs Report'), para 1.10, p. 12.

4   And government: consider the scandals surrounding the EU's own accounts ….

have declined in value, a few have gone bankrupt. But that is what should happen to corporations that fail to achieve their shareholders' objectives, or that act in ways which are incompatible with them. The scandals have provided no evidence either of market failure, or of any systemic breakdown of Anglo-American corporate governance.

Events since the first publication of *Corporate Governance: Accountability in the Marketplace* have therefore provided no reason to reject or modify the book's main theme, that the Anglo-American model of corporate governance is better than the alternatives at achieving the definitive goals of corporate governance.

This superiority has indeed been both enhanced and recognised by the main changes in international corporate governance since 1998. Particularly in the UK, what was 'best practice' in 1998 has come to be more prevalent; current best practice more closely resembles what is theoretically possible. And contrary to many expectations, the Anglo-American and other systems of corporate governance have not been converging to some middle ground. Rather, laws in the main jurisdictions usually considered as alternatives to the Anglo-American model – notably Germany and Japan – have moved those systems substantially closer to the Anglo-American model of corporate governance.

But the continuing superiority of the Anglo-American model does not justify complacency. Despite – or perhaps precisely because of – its prominent successes, the Anglo-American model remains under attack. Insufficiently understood and appreciated by its many beneficiaries, it is at risk of being undermined by frequent calls for government regulation; as will be argued in Chapter 7 below, even regulation that ostensibly supports the tenets of the Anglo-American model is normally counterproductive.

Regulatory initiatives have typically been directed not at strengthening the accountability of corporations to their shareholders, but at transforming corporations into agencies for promoting official social and economic policies. Even attempts to mitigate the genuine defects outlined in Chapter 4 below have typically undermined shareholders' abilities to hold their corporations to account. Particularly dangerous are the calls for regulatory enforcement of misguided notions of corporate social responsibility[5] and 'stakeholding'[6]. Were they enacted, they would undermine not only the Anglo-American system of corporate governance, but more fundamentally, the private property that is both a support for and a constituent of individual liberty.

Although the conceptual defence of the Anglo-American system of corporate governance offered in the first edition of *Corporate Governance: Accountability in the Marketplace* remains unaltered, the second edition contains one major change. To emphasise the fact that the corporate governance model being defended here is the one characteristic of the United Kingdom and the United States, and to highlight the fact that this model is being contrasted with the system typical of Germany, in the second edition it is called 'Anglo-American' rather than 'Anglo-Saxon'.

---

5   For an analysis of its fundamental errors, see Elaine Sternberg, *Just Business: Business Ethics in Action* ('*JB*'; 2nd edn, Oxford University Press, 2000; 1st edn, Little, Brown, London, 1994; Warner paperback, 1995), especially Chapters 3 and 10, and David Henderson, *Misguided Virtue: False Notions of Corporate Social Responsibility* (Institute of Economic Affairs, 2002; New Zealand Business Roundtable, June 2001); for an analysis of its context, see David Henderson, *Anti-Liberalism 2000: The Rise of New Millennium Collectivism*, the 30th Annual Wincott Lecture (Institute of Economic Affairs, 2001).

6   See Chapter 6 below.

AUTHOR'S PREFACE TO THE FIRST EDITION

Corporate Governance: Accountability in the Marketplace ('*CGAIM*') has two main objectives. First, it seeks to clarify exactly what corporate governance is. Understanding the meaning of corporate governance is a necessary prerequisite for undertaking most other projects concerning corporate governance. The basic concept is, nevertheless, seldom if ever investigated. *CGAIM* seeks to identify the essential nature of corporate governance, and to distinguish it from concepts with which it is frequently confused (Chapter 1).

The paper's second objective is to offer a very particular defence of the traditional Anglo-Saxon model of corporate governance. It seeks to show that the traditional Anglo-Saxon model is better suited than most commonly proposed alternatives for achieving the definitive purpose of corporate governance. *CGAIM* does this by first briefly describing the Anglo-Saxon model (Chapter 2), and then using a two part argument to defend it.

In Chapter 3, *CGAIM* shows that many of the criticisms levelled at the Anglo-Saxon model of corporate governance are misconceived, being based on fundamental misunderstandings of what corporations are and what can legitimately be expected of them. Such confusions are seldom recognised or addressed, because conventional approaches to corporate governance are typically legal or economic rather than theoretical and philosophical. *CGAIM* seeks to remedy that lack. It therefore provides a conceptual analysis of such issues as 'immoral' corporate conduct, takeovers, 'short-termism', remuneration, the role of auditors, and 'shareholder democracy'. Reflecting its conceptual approach, which is not limited geographically or temporally, the paper typically does not provide current examples of good or bad practice: its purpose is to explore the nature of corporate governance, not to judge specific companies.

The second part of *CGAIM*'s defence of the traditional Anglo-Saxon system comes from applying its strict understanding of corporate governance to evaluating alternative models of corporate governance. While recognising that the Anglo-Saxon system does have serious flaws (Chapter 4), *CGAIM* argues that the German and Japanese systems (Chapter 5) and the popular stakeholder doctrine (Chapter 6) and regulation (Chapter 7[1]) are considerably less capable of achieving the definitive purpose of corporate governance. Accordingly, the proper response to the defects of the Anglo-Saxon system is to find ways of correcting them (Chapter 8[2]), not to abandon the model altogether, as too many critics have advocated.

In focusing on its two fundamental themes – defining corporate governance, and showing how the definitive purpose of corporate governance is better served by the traditional Anglo-Saxon system than by the alternatives – *Corporate Governance: Accountability in the Marketplace* eschews many topics that are more customarily associated with the term 'corporate governance'. *CGAIM* is, for example, not a treatise on economics: it does not attempt to analyse the effects of corporate governance on wealth or on economic growth, on competitiveness or on access to capital markets.

---

1   Formerly part of Chapter 6.
2   Formerly Chapter 7.

Corporate Governance: Accountability in the Marketplace is also not, except incidentally, about history or law, psychology, sociology or politics. It does not seek to explain how and why corporations have developed, nor to survey the intricacies of company law, nor to evaluate recent corporate governance reports. It does not attempt to detail the various corporate governance systems that are employed worldwide, nor to evaluate their ability to promote either corporate performance or political objectives. *CGAIM* does not explore what might motivate investors to become active owners, nor what might motivate stakeholders to improve their productivity. Neither does it attempt to assess the damage done by different failures of corporate governance, nor to assign responsibility for them. *CGAIM* does not even consider how best to implement the various corrective measures that it itself identifies. Those are all interesting and important topics, but they are not the subject of this short book.

Significantly, *Corporate Governance: Accountability in the Marketplace* also does not seek to identify the corporate governance conditions of business success. Business is only one of the many activities that can be pursued using corporate form; it is a fundamental premise of *CGAIM* that businesses and corporations are categorially different. *CGAIM* may help to promote business success, but only incidentally ... by showing how it differs from corporate governance: as Aristotle pointed out many centuries ago, it is easier to hit a target whose identity and location are known.

Finally, *Corporate Governance: Accountability in the Marketplace* is only peripherally about business ethics. Business ethics, and in particular the relationship between business ethics and corporate governance, are subjects I discuss at length elsewhere.[3]

3   Sternberg, *JB, op. cit.*.

Corporate Governance:
Accountability in the Marketplace

Section 1
Conceptual Foundations

'Corporate governance' is a phrase which has become increasingly common in public debate. Disturbed by prominent examples of corporate wrongdoing and corporate collapse, concerned about high executive remuneration, and worried about 'short-termism' and firms' vulnerability to hostile takeovers, commentators have routinely prescribed better corporate governance as the cure. Unfortunately, their notions of improved corporate governance either have little to do with, or actively undermine, corporate governance properly understood.

The corporate governance challenge is not to bind businesses to advancing macroeconomic aims or industrial policy – that is not the function of corporate governance or the purpose of business. Nor is corporate governance about preventing businesses from pursuing profits or imposing 'social responsibilities' on business. Still less is it about elevating the claims of stakeholders over those of shareholders. Properly understood, corporate governance refers simply to ways of ensuring that a corporation's actions, agents, and assets are directed at the definitive corporate ends set by the corporation's shareholders.

However flawed current Anglo-American corporate governance mechanisms may be, the proper response is not to abandon accountability to owners, as so many prominent commentators have recommended. Nor is the answer to ape Germany or Japan, or to enshrine 'stakeholder theory', or to subject corporate functioning to still more stringent regulation. Rather, the solution is to improve the accountability of corporations to their ultimate owners. This can best be accomplished through a real market for corporate control, in which corporations compete for investment, and institutional investors for funds, in part on the degree of accountability they offer to their beneficial owners. The responsibility for corporate governance properly lies with corporate shareholders.

1 THE MEANING OF CORPORATE GOVERNANCE

Corporate governance is popularly thought to be at issue whenever questions arise about the conduct of large organisations. Indeed, the traditional Anglo-American model of corporate governance, identified loosely with Anglo-American individualism and 'short-termism', has been held responsible for many of the evils of the modern world, from psychic insecurity to the disintegration of the family.[1] Much of what is commonly taken to be criticism of corporate governance, however, actually deals with quite other matters. It is therefore essential to distinguish corporate governance from related topics with which it is frequently confused. Only then can the distinctively corporate governance issues – or the others – be properly addressed.

Corporate governance is not about the 'relationship of corporations to society'[2]. Without elucidation, that notion is so broad as to be virtually meaningless; it might refer to business history or

---

1   Stephen Davies, 'Short-termism and the State We're In', Institute of Directors Economic Research Paper, 1996, pp. 5–6.

2   See, for example, Martin Dickson, 'Sharpening up the cutting edge', *Financial Times*, 15 July 1996, p. 10. According to the EU Green Paper *Promoting a European framework for corporate social responsibility* (European Commission Directorate-General for Employment and Social Affairs, Unit EMPL/D.1, July 2001, Concepts Annex, p. 27; henceforth '*EUcsr*'), corporate governance is 'a set of relationships between a company's management, its board, its shareholders and other stakeholders.'.

industrial sociology or commercial law. Nor is corporate governance about the regulation of corporations in the interests of society: regulation backed by the force of law is the subject of civil government, not corporate governance. Equally, corporate governance is not about 'the creation of a healthy economy through the development of business operations that operate for the long term and compete successfully in the world economy.'[3] Corporate governance is neither the study of economics nor the promotion of enterprise.

Conversely, corporate governance is not just about what are sometimes called 'hygiene' matters – administrative rules that are imposed on corporations independent of shareholders' wishes or corporate circumstances. The aim of corporate governance should be to improve the achievement of shareholders' objectives, not to interfere with corporate operations. Corporate governance is also not, despite the definition used by the Cadbury Committee[4] and the Hampel Report[5], simply 'the system by which companies are directed and controlled'. That characterisation could as easily refer to the law, or the market or politics.

Properly understood, corporate governance is something very limited and very specific. Throughout this discussion, corporate governance will refer exclusively to *ways of ensuring that corporate actions, agents and assets are directed at achieving the corporate objectives*[6] *established by the corporation's shareholders*. Although this

---

3 Martin Lipton and Steven A. Rosenblum, 'A New System of Corporate Governance: the Quinquennial Election of Directors', *University of Chicago Law Review*, 58 (1), winter 1991, pp. 187–253, as abstracted.

4 In its *Report on the Financial Aspects of Corporate Governance* (Gee Publishing, December 1992), paragraph 2.5.

5 Hampel Committee on Corporate Governance, *Final Report*, Gee Publishing, January 1998, para. 1.15.

6 For an explanation of what is meant by 'corporate objectives' see the section on 'The corporate form' in Chapter 2 below.

definition excludes many interesting concerns, it provides a framework for the rigorous exploration of questions that are central to the proper functioning and control of corporations. In particular, clearly identifying corporate governance shows that most of the criticisms that have been made of the traditional Anglo-American system of corporate governance are, at best, beside the point. They are criticisms of particular corporate purposes or outcomes[7] rather than of corporate governance *per se*. Or they are based on a misunderstanding of what a corporation is, and what it should do.

Such misunderstandings may also prompt objections to this definition of corporate governance. It may be protested that this definition does not refer to the conditions of business success, or the role of stakeholders (however they are defined) in achieving it. Such criticisms are, however, based on a fundamental misunderstanding of the nature of the corporation, and a failure to recognise that the corporate form can be used for objectives other than business. The distinctive features of corporations, and how they differ from businesses, will be discussed below, in Chapter 2. Here it is sufficient to note two key points. First, the reason why corporate governance refers solely to shareholders, and not to stakeholders[8], is because corporations are the property of their shareholders in aggregate; corporations are owned by, and properly structured to serve the objectives of, their shareholders. Second, accepting the proposed definition of corporate governance does not diminish either the importance of stakeholders in achieving the corporate objectives, or the need to treat stakeholders ethically[9]. It simply

7   For a general discussion of 'teleopathy', getting the ends wrong, see Sternberg, *JB, op. cit.*, especially pp. 4, 203–5.

8   For a discussion of the concept and its definition, see Chapter 6 below.

9   For a discussion of what ethical treatment of stakeholders means, see Chapter 3 below.

recognises the difference between means and ends.

There are several advantages to the strict definition of corporate governance. First, it makes explicit something which should be obvious, but which is all too often overlooked: corporate governance is about *corporations*. It is remarkable – in both senses of the word – how often popular and political discussions of corporate governance are not about corporations, but either about other forms of organisation, or about businesses.

Second, the strict definition highlights the fact that corporate governance necessarily involves three elements: agents, principals and outcomes. A particular group of people – corporate directors – are accountable to a second group – the corporate owners – for the achievement of a designated outcome – the corporate objective. Thus, for example, in business corporations, directors are properly accountable *to* shareholders *for* maximising shareholder value.

This often overlooked feature of corporate governance provides the solution to a major dispute that flared when the Hampel Report was published, and which persists: should corporate governance focus on corporate accountability or on corporate performance? The dispute is based on a false dichotomy. In a business corporation, directors' accountability *to* shareholders is not in any way opposed to the directors' responsibility *for* maximising shareholder value. Quite the contrary. Both principals and purposes are essential for specifying the accountability that is central to corporate governance.

A third advantage of the strict definition is that it helps to identify corporate governance mechanisms: they are the means by which corporate agents are held accountable to the shareholders for achieving the corporate objectives. The governance system of a corporation consists of directors' powers and duties, corporate elections, and rules of approval, authorisation and accountability. Corporations do, of course, have other features that are essential for their functioning: they need capital and labour, supplies and management. Corporations are also subject to external constraints in the form of market conditions, and to external controls imposed by the laws and regulations of the jurisdictions in which they operate. But such external factors can only function through the corporation's internal governance mechanisms. Without the internal, structural governance mechanisms, a corporation can no more comply with governmental directives than it can with the owners' wishes. Corporate governance mechanisms are essential means for achieving corporate ends.

Corporate governance and corporate purposes

One common source of confusion in discussions of corporate governance is the failure to distinguish the ends of a corporation – its legitimately constituted purpose or objectives – from the mechanisms used to keep agents tied to those ends. Unless they are properly differentiated, defects may be incorrectly identified, and corporate energies misdirected. Efforts that should be devoted to improving corporate performance may, in the name of corporate governance, be diverted instead to activities that undermine the corporate objectives.

Many supposed criticisms of the traditional Anglo-American system of corporate governance do not concern any failure of corporate governance mechanisms to hold corporate agents to corporate ends: they are instead criticisms of specific outcomes. Notable examples include protests that the Anglo-American governance system allows corporate collapses, or encourages 'short-termism', that it permits redundancies and accommodates wide variations in remuneration.

Often the real target is the activity of business as such. Many critics denounce traditional Anglo-American corporate governance simply because it permits using corporate assets to maximise owner value; they would prefer those resources to be devoted instead to some form of 'social responsibility', 'stakeholder' benefit or community welfare. Regardless of whether the end they favour is environmental purity, social stability or guaranteed employment, however, such critics are attacking a particular corporate end, not corporate governance. Such complaints are comparable to claiming that automotive steering mechanisms are at fault because too many motorists head for the seaside on bank holidays.

The way to address such *end-related* criticisms is to make clear that the real target is not corporate governance, but the specific outcomes. Only when those outcomes are identified, can their merits be properly examined, and sensible decisions made about whether the criticisms of those outcomes are justified; that exercise is attempted in Chapter 3 below.

Corporate governance systems are also subject to *functional* criticism. Functional criticisms of corporate governance are independent of the corporate purposes: they relate to the ability of corporate governance mechanisms to keep the corporation directed at any official corporate purpose, whatever it might be. Charges that directors are insufficiently independent of management but too independent of shareholders are criticisms of this kind. So are complaints that it is difficult for shareholders to nominate directors or put motions on the agenda for general meetings. The way to address such criticisms is to identify the source of the defective functioning, and to investigate whether there are ways in which the defects might be remedied without causing still more serious problems to arise elsewhere in the system; that exercise is attempted in Chapters 4 and 8 below.

Corporate governance contrasted with government

Just as many misguided criticisms of corporate governance arise from confusing corporate governance with corporate objectives, others come from confusing corporate governance with government. Most notably, this sort of confusion leads to two quite separate kinds of end-related criticism: those which criticise corporations for not achieving public policy objectives, and those which reproach corporations for not giving their stakeholders the rights and privileges commonly associated with citizenship.

Public policy objectives are distinguished from private objectives by being embodied in government regulation or legislation. Because they are backed by the use of the state's coercive power, public policy objectives are legitimately chosen and implemented only by those who are publicly accountable to the electorate. It would be inappropriate to allow corporations, which are properly accountable only to their shareholders, to assume governmental powers. Being subject to the law of the land, corporations are, of course, obliged to comply with it. But their responsibility for achieving public policy objectives is no greater than that of any other person or type of organisation.

A second reason why it is inappropriate to criticise corporations for not achieving public policy objectives, is because those objectives are only questionably legitimate even for governments. On the classical liberal doctrine of government, power is accorded to government only for use in establishing and maintaining a framework in which private ends can peaceably be pursued.[10] Promoting economic growth and social welfare are therefore not legitimate government functions. Moreover, even if such objectives were valid for governments, they would still not be valid for most corporations. It is theoretically possible for a corporation to adopt, for example, reducing local unemployment as its definitive purpose. That objective is, however, only incidentally compatible with other corporate objectives, including being a business[11]. To the extent that existing corporations have business as their official purpose, they cannot substitute a public policy objective for it without violating their very reason for being.

Inferring from governments to corporate governance is misleading even when government is merely a night watchman. Because the objective of the classical liberal state is simply to protect citizens' life and (negative) liberty[12], the constitution of such a state will systematically impede all government action not directed at those essential functions. Similar structural limitations would be unsuitable for corporations: unlike governments, corporations do

10   Like actual commercial organisations, actual governments do much more in practice, and arrogate to themselves diverse functions and objectives. That they do so, however, in no way undermines the correctness of the analysis. For a fuller exposition of this notion of the role of government, see, for example, Friedrich A. Hayek, *The Road to Serfdom*, University of Chicago Press, 1944, especially Chapter VI, and Milton Friedman, *Capitalism and Freedom*, University of Chicago Press, 1962, especially Chapter II. For its philosophical underpinnings, see, e.g., Thomas Hobbes, *Leviathan*, and the works of Michael J. Oakeshott, especially *On Human Conduct*, Oxford University Press, 1975, Section II.

11   Sternberg, *JB, op. cit.*, and 'A Teleological Approach to Business Ethics', in W. W. Gasparski and Leo V. Ryan (eds), *Human Action in Business*, Praxiology, vol. 5, Transaction Publishers, 1996, pp. 51–64.

12   Isaiah Berlin, *Two Concepts of Liberty*, An Inaugural Lecture delivered before the University of Oxford on 31 October 1958, Clarendon Press, 1958.

have legitimate substantive objectives, the corporate purposes. Corporations therefore need a governance system that facilitates, rather than obstructs, the achievement of those ends.

It is equally unreasonable to criticise corporate governance for not protecting stakeholders' 'rights'. Although members of society do not lose whatever natural or legal rights they already have by becoming stakeholders of corporations, the only rights that they have in their capacity as stakeholders are those conferred on them by law or specific contractual agreements. Stakeholder theory will be criticised in detail in Chapter 6 below; the clarification of the meaning and implications of 'shareholder democracy' in Chapter 3 below will show other ways in which the parallel with government fails. Here it is sufficient to note that stakeholders as such have no special rights. Accordingly, it is not a valid criticism of corporate governance systems that they fail to support them. Once again, confounding corporate governance with government only causes confusion.

There is, nevertheless, one fundamental way in which corporate governance is ordinarily dependent on government. As currently constituted, corporations are normally created in accordance with the laws of some jurisdiction or other; those laws define the local corporate form and its general characteristics.[13] All dealings with corporations must therefore take into account the laws and regulations of the jurisdictions in which they are constituted. Whenever possible, however, this discussion will focus on the conceptual features that characterise all corporations, rather than on their varying legal forms.

---

13   This does not mean that corporations are necessarily 'creatures of the law'. Organisational forms affording limited liability to their owners, and recognised as having an existence independent of those owners, could be created by private contract; although such arrangements are now largely crowded out by regulatory restrictions, they are possible in principle.

2 THE TRADITIONAL ANGLO-AMERICAN THEORY OF CORPORATE GOVERNANCE

The notion of corporate governance has now been differentiated from corporate purposes and from government. Before criticisms of, and alternatives to, the traditional Anglo-American theory of corporate governance can be sensibly evaluated, however, it is appropriate to clarify exactly what that theory is. Understanding the traditional theory of corporate governance in turn requires understanding what corporations[1] are, and what is distinctive about them.

The corporate form

The first and most fundamental characteristic of a corporation is that it is an artificial person, with assets, liabilities and purposes distinct from those of its owners, the shareholders. Unlike the other organisational forms commonly used to constitute businesses – notably sole proprietorships and partnerships – a corporation has an independent legal existence, and is thus capable of enjoying perpetual life. Corporate debts are the responsibility of the corporation, not its shareholders; shareholders' liability for such debts is normally limited to the value of their shareholdings in the corporation.

---

1   Unless otherwise specified, 'corporation' here refers to a company limited by shares.

Though it is a separate legal person, the corporation is, however, a *slave*. The corporation has owners, the shareholders, who determine its purposes and who are ultimately entitled to control it. In exchange for contributing capital and bearing the residual risk of the corporation to the extent of the value of their shares, the shareholders ordinarily have a permanent, proportional participation in the corporation's profits (via dividends), its prospects (via capital gains), and its ultimate control (via voting rights). Corporations can[2] be terminated if their shareholders wish: shareholders can cause their corporation to be acquired by or merged into another corporation, or to be wound up.

Corporate purposes

Originally chartered only for special purposes, corporations are now routinely created, but are still differentiated by the ends for which they are formed and which they characteristically pursue.[3] Subject only to what the law allows, the purposes for which corporations are established can be anything their owners choose. The Joseph Rowntree Reform Trust Limited is a charitable corporation; the London School of Economics is an educational one.[4]

---

2   Subject to regulation in the relevant jurisdictions.

3   Such ends would be abolished if the UK government had its way; see The Company Law Review Steering Group, *Modern Company Law for a Competitive Economy, the Strategic Framework*, February 1999, Articles 5.3.18–19, pp. 77–8 and *The Final Report*, June 2001, Vol. I, Article 9.10, p. 215.

4   Both are corporations limited by guarantee, the form often favoured by non-business organisations.

'Not-for-profit' corporations are common in the United States; in Japan, both charities[5] and gangsters[6] incorporate.

Most significantly, the corporate form need not be used for a business purpose. Contrary to popular opinion, not all corporations are businesses, and not all businesses are corporations[7]. By number if not by importance, more businesses are sole proprietorships and partnerships than are corporate in form. Business is the activity of maximising long-term owner value by selling goods or services[8]; that definitive objective may be pursued using a variety of organisational forms. A corporation, in contrast, is a particular organisational form, which is compatible with diverse objectives.

Corporations are so commonly used for business purposes, however, and so many prominent businesses are incorporated, that most commentators treat 'business' and 'corporation' as synonyms. This is, nevertheless, a serious mistake. It can lead people who reject the business purpose to a needless rejection of the benefits of corporate form. Conversely, it can lead those adopting corporate form for non-business purposes to focus inappropriately on wealth maximisation rather than their proper objectives of, e.g., education or healthcare. Confusing businesses with corpor-

---

5   In 1998, the Diet passed the Special Nonprofit Activities Promotion Law, which created a new category of incorporated organisation known as the 'Special Activities Nonprofit Legal Person'. Robert Pekkanen and Karla Simon, 'Taxation of Not-for-Profit Organisations and Their Donors in Japan: Is this Tax Reform or Not?', *The International Journal of Not-for-Profit Law*, 4(2), May 2002.

6   See 'Tycoons of crime', *The Economist*, 29 February 1992, p. 62.

7   Corporate form is to business what book form is to the novel: common, but neither necessary nor sufficient. Although novels have conventionally been written and presented in the form of bound volumes of paper, they can equally well be created and distributed on audio tape, computer disks or other media.

8   For a detailed justification and explanation of this characterisation of business, see Sternberg, *JB, op. cit.*, especially Chapter 2.

ations can also lead judgements that are meant for all business to exclude the very large segment of the business universe that is not incorporated, and inappropriately to include charitable and other non-business corporations.

If the corporate purpose cannot be assumed to be business, what is it? The corporate purpose is not the same as the purposes and objectives of the shareholders. Both in their private lives and in their capacity as investors, shareholders can have objectives that are as diverse as they are. Whether individual or institutional, shareholders typically have time horizons, levels of sophistication, risk/reward profiles, and levels of dedication to and resources for enforcing their own interests that differ significantly from each other.

However diverse the objectives of the shareholders may be, the corporate purpose is nevertheless easy to identify: it is that which is set out in the corporation's Memorandum of Association or comparable constitutional document. Whether the corporate purpose is framed broadly or narrowly, it is that constitutional purpose which is relevant to corporate governance. Unless otherwise specified, all references in this book to 'official' corporate purposes or objectives, and to 'shareholders' purposes' or 'shareholders' objectives' refer to this constitutional purpose; references to 'shareholders' interests' refer to their interests in having the constitutional purpose achieved.

It may perhaps be objected that such constitutional purposes are irrelevant. Most corporations have purposes that are framed so widely as to permit them to do almost anything; they are so wide, precisely to leave corporations and their agents free to act without constant reference to the shareholders.[9] Moreover, however

---

9   As will be suggested below, in Chapter 8, narrower corporate purposes may be one way of improving corporate governance.

broad their official purposes are, most corporations do much else besides: for example, they collect taxes and support charities and constitute social environments. That they do so, however, does not diminish the importance of the official objective.

The official corporate purpose is important because it creates expectations and establishes limits. If a corporation solicits stakeholder participation on the basis of being a business, it creates legitimate expectations that it will be run as a business, and not as a family or a charity. Similarly, if a charity collects funds for famine relief, but uses them for arts sponsorship, contributors have a legitimate grievance. They do so, because corporate purposes determine which activities are legitimate for the corporation. Many activities are prerequisites, concomitants or consequences of the official corporate purposes; such ancillary activities are appropriate and sometimes necessary. To the extent that corporate activities are extraneous to the official purposes, however, they may not properly be pursued: they violate the corporation's very reason for being. And in many jurisdictions, they are *ultra vires*[10].

The requirements of corporate governance

The need for corporate governance arises because the advantages of corporate form are typically achieved at the cost of separating ownership from operational control. When management is detached from ownership, and especially when ownership is dif-

---

10 Though not in the UK, if the UK government has its way. *Ultra vires* was significantly weakened by the Companies Act 1989, and would be eliminated altogether by the proposed reforms of company law. See *Modernising Company Law*, Cm 5553–1, July 2002, Vol. 2, *A New Companies Bill: Draft Clauses*, Part I, Chapter 1, Clause 1, Section 5, p. 1, and Part III, Notes on Draft Clauses, p. 59.

fuse, it is possible for managers to run a corporation to serve their own ends. Mechanisms are therefore needed for ensuring that corporate actions, agents and assets are devoted to achieving the corporate purpose established by the shareholders. Whether that purpose is business or charity or education, the aim of corporate governance is to make sure that it is the shareholders' stipulated objective that governs the corporation and all its actions and agents.

The key concept in corporate governance is accountability. Accountability means that individuals and institutions are answerable for what they do: they must account to others for their conduct and for their use of resources. Two sorts of accountability are critical for corporate governance: the accountability of directors to shareholders, and the accountability of corporate employees and other corporate agents to the corporation. What directors and all corporate agents are accountable for, is achieving the corporate purposes. A successful model of corporate governance must be compatible with, and provide mechanisms for, both these sorts of accountability. Because other corporate agents are normally held accountable to the corporation by the directors, the accountability of directors to shareholders is crucial to both sorts of accountability; it will therefore be the focus of the following discussion.

Corporate governance mechanisms

The key mechanisms for ensuring accountability in Anglo-American corporate governance are the powers and responsibilities of directors, the requirement that directors report periodically to the shareholders, and the requirement that certain corporate appointments and types of corporate action receive explicit shareholder authorisation. These internal structures receive ancillary support from audits and the possibility of takeovers. The efficacy or otherwise of these mechanisms will be addressed below, in Chapter 4; this chapter simply seeks to identify what the mechanisms are.

Directors[11]

The powers and obligations of the board of directors are the most obvious means by which corporations are controlled. The board's definitive responsibility is to direct the corporation to achieving the corporate purposes established by the shareholders. To that end, the board must, *inter alia*, set policy in accordance with shareholder objectives, authorise key corporate decisions, appoint senior executives and auditors, nominate directors (in some jurisdictions), monitor corporate and executive performance, and determine executive remuneration. The board must also establish and monitor internal control systems to ensure that corporate actions which are not taken directly by the board are nonetheless legal and are directed at achieving the corporate objectives.

The role of a director is conceptually different from that of a manager or executive. The responsibility of a director is to direct the corporation, to ensure that it pursues the constitutional objectives set by the shareholders. The responsibility of executives, in contrast, is to execute the directors' strategy. In motoring terms, the shareholders choose the destination, the directors determine the route, and the executives drive the car. Though in practice the directors of firms are often the executive managers of those same

---

11   See also Sternberg, *JB, op. cit.*, especially pp. 226–36.

firms, the responsibilities they have as operating executives and as directors are conceptually distinct.

The role of the director incorporates elements of representative and steward, trustee and watchdog[12]. As an artificial person, a corporation needs actual people – directors – to represent it. But though the directors represent the corporation, the corporation is the property of the shareholders in aggregate. Directors therefore have a fiduciary responsibility to use the corporate assets and their corporate powers to achieve the corporate objectives of the shareholders. To ensure that those corporate purposes are achieved, directors must oversee the actions of corporate management. Like watchdogs, directors are responsible for identifying problems and raising the alert. Unlike canine watchdogs, however, directors are also responsible for diagnosing and correcting what is wrong.

For directors to perform their role properly, they need specific abilities and character traits that are significantly different from those often supposed. A business director must, of course, understand very clearly how owner value is maximised. But such understanding requires critical intelligence, not 'clubbability' or having influential contacts, professional credentials, specific business experience, or academic degrees.

The essential qualities of good directors are those which enable them to ask the questions necessary for safeguarding the owners' interests, and to get and evaluate and act on the answers. The relevant qualities are those of a good steward: loyalty, integrity, sound judgement and moral courage. Directors' loyalty must be to the corporate purpose, not to the managers, the employees, the

---

12   This is a conceptual analysis of the role of the director; directors' actual legal status depends on the laws of particular jurisdictions.

customers, to any particular stakeholding group or any corporate function[13] or even to any particular shareholders; the role of the director is to pursue the corporate objectives, not to promote sectional interests. Sound judgement involves knowing what counts as achievement of the corporate goal, and appreciating what is likely to bring it about; directors must be able to estimate the long-term consequences of corporate actions. And they must know what information they need to make such assessments and how to get it.

Directors must understand when and how to challenge management's actions, and when to bring matters directly to the attention of the shareholders[14]. They must also be ready to act on that understanding. A director who cannot cope with confrontation, and is not prepared to ask hard questions and demand satisfactory answers, is unqualified for the job. Directors must scrutinise actual and proposed corporate activities; they must allow only those projects and policies which advance the definitive corporate end.

To perform their essential functions effectively, directors need independence, information and access to corporate resources. Genuine independence requires that the directors' appointment and access to information and advice be independent of the company's management.[15] It is usually easier for a director to view the acts of the managers critically if he is not one of them himself, if he does not share their vested interest in defending the *status quo*.

---

13 UK titles, e.g., 'finance director', 'marketing director', are misleading: although there may well be some division of labour within a board, and that division may reflect the individuals' executive roles, the directorial responsibilities of all directors are the same.

14 Which may in some jurisdictions count as a breach of company confidentiality ....

15 Different ways of securing directors' independence of management are discussed in Chapter 8 below.

This is the main justification for the existence of non-executive or 'independent' directors, and for having key board committees consist mainly or exclusively of non-executives.

Accounts

Like the role of directors, the function of the accounts is often misunderstood. Contrary to popular opinion, the fundamental financial mechanism for corporate governance is not the audit, but the requirement to report periodically to shareholders. Directors must account to the shareholders for their conduct of the company and their use of company assets and resources. Though such reports to shareholders can take various forms, the annual financial accounts are the most prominent. The annual report and accounts should give shareholders the information they need to evaluate the performance of the corporation and that of the directors as stewards. It is these accounts which are typically subject to auditing, and which are normally presented to the shareholders for their approval[16] at the Annual General Meeting. The function of the audit is simply to check whether the accounts have been compiled in such a way as to give 'a true and fair' picture.

General meetings and votes

The Annual General Meeting ('AGM') is a key mechanism for keeping directors accountable to shareholders. Typically required

---

16 In UK company law, this is not a requirement; consider the (rapidly withdrawn) attempt by Commercial Union to remove the right of its shareholders to vote on the report and accounts; Christopher Adams, 'CU backs down on plan to deny vote on accounts', *Financial Times*, 4 April 1997, p. 1.

by company law and corporations' constitutional documents, the AGM provides a periodic opportunity for the shareholders to review the performance of their company. The AGM is when the shareholders officially receive the accounts, appoint directors and auditors, declare dividends, and vote on major issues. Shareholders can remove offending directors, and exercise control by authorising, or refusing to authorise, certain kinds of corporate activity, notably the raising of capital.

Shareholders also exercise control by voting at Extraordinary General Meetings ('EGM's), which are called[17] when subjects of importance to the future of the corporation need to be decided. EGMs are, for example, typically called to allow shareholders to vote on whether to accept takeover bids made for their company.

Takeovers

Although takeovers are commonly considered to be the ultimate corporate governance mechanism, their nature and function are often misunderstood. A takeover occurs when one company acquires another by buying up its shares. Takeovers differ from ordinary purchases of shares because the buyer acquires a controlling interest, and typically uses it to change the board and the management of the acquired company.

Takeovers' ability to influence corporate conduct depends largely on the tendency of new owners to replace boards of directors and senior management. The mere threat of a takeover may therefore serve to improve corporate governance: realising that

---

17   In the UK by directors, though under Section 368 of the Companies Act 1985, 10 per cent of the shareholders, or holders of 10 per cent of the issued share capital, have the power to require directors to call an EGM.

poor performance can cost them their jobs, managements and boards may be motivated to try harder to achieve the shareholders' objectives. When takeovers actually occur, they normally replace directors and managers by replacing the owners. Accordingly, to the extent that market information is imperfect, those who gain from the new regime are typically the acquirors who appoint the replacement team, not the selling shareholders.

Selling shareholders do nevertheless stand to benefit from takeovers. First, the price they get for their shares is typically greater than if there had been no takeover bid. Other things being equal, when the number of shares stays constant, but there is substantial new demand, the price of those shares will rise. Moreover, since bidders normally have to pay a premium in order to secure control, sellers normally get more than the market price for their shares. Finally, once the target company is 'in play' as a takeover possibility, other bidders may enter the contest. A 'white knight' may appear to protect the target from an unwanted bidder; other potential purchasers, alerted to the possibilities of the target company by the public takeover bid, may also decide to try their hand. Either way, the competition can lead to the target company's shares being bid up and commanding substantially higher prices than they did before the bid commenced. So even when the target company's shareholders give up their ownership of the company, they can gain substantially from a takeover.

Useful though they are, however, takeovers are a derivative form of corporate governance. They rely for their effectiveness on the ability of the new owners to change the directors and conduct of the firm. The central mechanisms of corporate governance are the powers and responsibilities of directors, the requirement that directors report periodically to the shareholders, and the requirement that certain corporate actions receive explicit shareholder authorisation. The next two chapters will examine common criticisms of the Anglo-American corporate governance system, showing that while some are justified, many are spurious.

Section 2
Common Criticisms

3 COMMON CRITICISMS: SPURIOUS

The traditional Anglo-American system of corporate governance is liable to many valid criticisms; some will be addressed in
Chapter 4 below. The criticisms that are most commonly levelled
against it, however, are wholly spurious: they reflect confusions
that are both widespread and fundamental. Like 'When did you
stop beating your wife?', such challenges need to be unpacked
before they can be properly answered. This chapter aims simply
to expose such conceptual confusions; it does not seek either to
assess the damage they have done, or to assign blame for their per-
petration.

One especially pernicious complaint that needs corrective
analysis, is the charge that the traditional Anglo-American system of corporate governance promotes various sorts of immoral
conduct. Refuting such charges requires not just examining the
particulars of each claim, but more fundamentally, examining
what it means for corporate conduct to be moral. That is a large
and important topic, and one that is the subject of a separate
book[1]. For the purposes of this discussion, however, it is sufficient
to make two main points.

First, it is important to highlight the absurdity of one extremely

---

1   See Sternberg, *JB, op. cit.*, for a detailed analysis of the ethical conditions of busi-
    ness and, more generally, corporations.

widespread view about what counts as ethical or socially responsible conduct, either by corporations or by individuals in their corporate capacities. This is the belief that being socially responsible or ethical in corporate terms requires pursuing some social welfare or environmental or religious end in place of the corporate purpose. According to this popular notion, the way for a corporation to be moral is to devote its resources to fulfilling 'social responsibilities'[2] or stakeholder interests rather than to pursuing its definitive end. This view is, however, literally absurd[3]: it makes not pursuing the corporate purpose the condition of achieving that purpose ethically or responsibly. This oxymoronic notion is, nevertheless, what underlies many standard criticisms of traditional Anglo-American corporate governance.

If pursuing 'social responsibilities' is not what makes corporate conduct ethical, what does? The answer is simple. Corporate conduct is ethical if it is directed at the corporate objective and respects 'distributive justice' and 'ordinary decency'[4]. These ethical principles are just the ones that must be satisfied for corporations and their long-term objectives to be possible. Because long-term views require confidence in a future, and confidence requires trust, the conditions of trust must be observed. Equally, corporations presuppose ownership and therefore respect for property rights. In order not to be ultimately self-defeating, corporate activities must therefore be conducted with honesty, fairness, the absence of physical violence and coercion, and a

---

2   For a fuller analysis of 'social responsibility', see *ibid.*, pp. 257–60.

3   Except for those (rare, if indeed existent) corporations whose definitive end is simply to fulfil 'social responsibilities'.

4   For a comprehensive explanation, justification and application of these concepts, see *ibid.*, especially Chapter 3.

presumption in favour of legality. Collectively, these constraints embody what may be called '*ordinary decency*'.

Furthermore, because a corporation has a definitive purpose, it should encourage contributions to that purpose rather than to others. Accordingly, classical '*distributive justice*' is essential. Just as 'ordinary decency' is distinct from vague notions of 'niceness', this concept of justice has nothing to do with modern attempts to redistribute income on ideological grounds. What distributive justice means is simply that those who contribute most to achieving the objective of the organisation deserve most from the organisation. That principle applies to all the rewards a corporation has to distribute: it covers not just payments and promotions, but also praise and prizes and – significantly – responsibilities. Though the term 'distributive justice' may be unfamiliar, the underlying concept is widely recognised. It is implicit in the commonly accepted view that productive workers deserve more than shirkers; when properly structured, both performance-related pay and promotion on merit are expressions of distributive justice.[5]

The constraints of distributive justice and ordinary decency cover both the ways in which the corporate purpose is pursued and the corporate end itself. While organisations with clearly illegal ends (providing assassins for hire, for example) are unlikely to be allowed to incorporate, it is possible to imagine corporate ends that are vague enough to pass muster ('providing troubleshooting services', perhaps) while accommodating unethical objectives. Immoral corporate purposes are, however, largely hypothetical. Most corporations are intended to be businesses. But contrary to popular opinion, there is nothing intrinsically

---

5   Distributive justice is about objectives and merit, not motivation; see Sternberg, *JB, op. cit.*, p. ix.

unethical about the definitive business objective of maximising long-term owner value by selling goods or services.[6] There are undoubtedly ways of doing business that are unethical, because they violate distributive justice or ordinary decency, or conflict with other objectives that have ethical priority in particular circumstances. But there is nothing intrinsically unethical about business itself or business corporations.

The essential point is that corporations are ethical when they pursue their definitive objectives subject to distributive justice and ordinary decency. If a corporation is not directed at achieving its definitive objective, it violates its reason for being; if that definitive corporate purpose or the manner of its pursuit violate distributive justice or ordinary decency, the corporation is not ethical.

'Immoral' takeovers permitted[7]

Confusion about what constitutes ethical corporate conduct underlies one of the most frequent criticisms of the traditional Anglo-American system of corporate governance, that it allows 'immoral' takeovers. The charge's central presupposition, that takeovers are intrinsically immoral, is, however, simply false. That will be demonstrated by examining in detail the main reasons why takeovers are thought to be unethical, and showing those reasons to be defective. Since the arguments against takeovers are usually directed at business corporations, the refutation will also be framed in terms of business.

---

6   See *ibid.*, pp. 57–61.

7   This section draws heavily on *ibid.*, pp. 170–9.

Stakeholder upheaval

One common charge is that takeovers are by their very nature destructive of the interests of stakeholders: they eliminate jobs, threaten communities, disrupt relationships with suppliers and customers. In evaluating such criticisms, the crucial point is that not all stakeholders' interests are equally legitimate. The purpose of a corporation is to achieve the official objective of its shareholders; the interests of the other stakeholders are relevant to the corporation only insofar as they contribute to that definitive end.[8] The disruption of stakeholders may pose matters of serious business concern to an acquiror; such disturbances may, if severe enough, even raise questions of public policy. But the mere fact that stakeholders are disturbed is irrelevant to assessing the morality of takeovers. The ethical status of takeovers, like that of all other corporate activities, is a function of whether they respect distributive justice and ordinary decency while aiming to achieve the corporate purposes.

Corporations have no right to continued existence if their shareholders decide otherwise; equally, stakeholder relationships are not eternal. Despite the widespread British belief to the contrary, it can even be a good thing – for business, for the economy, for employees' own self-esteem and income – when workers are released from unproductive employment, and freed to make a greater contribution to long-term owner value elsewhere. Change is positively beneficial when the alternative is death or decay.

Whether the disruptions caused by takeovers are moral depends on how they are handled. By precipitating major changes, takeovers provide significant occasions for behaving badly. But

8   Or have been accepted through contractual arrangements.

opportunities for misconduct are, unfortunately, provided by any major source of change, be it growth or restructuring or regulation. However unfortunate the bad business behaviour associated with takeovers may be, takeovers themselves are merely the occasion for such lapses; they are not the cause. As methods of transferring control, takeovers are no more intrinsically immoral than elections.

Reversal of fortune

But perhaps the problem isn't simply that takeovers cause change, but that they replace 'pillars of the community' with 'ruthless asset strippers'. Takeovers, it is claimed, undermine the very foundations of society, because they allow smaller companies and relative unknowns to gain control of major businesses. But there is no reason why they shouldn't. Substantial power inversions no doubt come as an unpleasant shock to those who are toppled, but they are not intrinsically immoral. What determines whether a particular change of business control is ethical is, as always, simply whether it is compatible with maximising long-term owner value subject to respecting distributive justice and ordinary decency.

The possibility of reverse takeovers, in which a smaller company takes over a larger one, can in fact be positively beneficial, both to the businesses involved and the communities in which they are situated. Power that cannot be challenged is more likely to ignore ethical constraints; by helping to keep large businesses accountable, takeovers and the threat of takeovers can perform an essential ethical service.

Breach of trust

A more serious charge against takeovers is that they transfer wealth to shareholders by violating implicit contracts with other stakeholders[9]. Businesses often lead their stakeholders to expect that certain sorts of behaviour will be rewarded over the long term. The reliable supplier expects a chance to match competitors' bids, the faithful employee expects job security, the important customer expects flexibility on credit terms. The charge is that takeovers divert the expected rewards from the stakeholders who have earned them to the shareholders.

Since honouring obligations is a crucial part of observing ordinary decency, the accusation of breach of trust is a grave one. For such a charge to be valid, however, three conditions would have to be satisfied. The specific agreements entered into by the target would have to have been legitimate arrangements. They would have to have been wrongly breached. And for takeovers to be condemned as intrinsically unethical, such violations of trust would have to be a necessary feature of takeovers. To what extent do takeovers satisfy these conditions?

The most important point to note is that not all undertakings are legitimate for a corporation, precisely because a corporation has an overriding obligation to achieve its definitive objective. All corporate stakeholders have a responsibility to understand what the corporate objective is, and to be wary of making or accepting counterproductive undertakings in their corporate capacities. Ordinary decency requires that a corporation not encourage inappropriate

---

9   See Andrei Shliefer and Laurence Summers, 'Breach of Trust in Hostile Takeovers', in Alan Auerbach, (ed.), *Corporate Takeovers: Causes and Consequences*, University of Chicago Press, 1988.

expectations in its stakeholders. And having encouraged realistic ones, a corporation should not disappoint them without good reason and explanation.

Far from being a necessary element of takeovers, breach of trust is likely to damage the ensuing corporation and render the takeover unworkable. Normally, a corporation will benefit from violating undertakings only if those undertakings themselves violated the corporate purpose, distributive justice or ordinary decency. Unethical breaches do take place, of course. Sadly, however, they occur rather more often in the course of ordinary business than as a result of acquisitions; many an incumbent manager has benefited from unethically exploiting the loyalty and trust of his staff.

Misallocation of resources

Another common charge against takeovers is that they transfer resources from productive enterprises into power games. Time, money, energy and attention that should be devoted to capital investment, to long-term research and development, and to managing the corporation generally, are, it is alleged, diverted into pursuing or repelling wasteful takeover bids, and to paying off the vast amounts of debt often incurred in doing so. On the surface, this seems a compelling criticism: if takeovers were intrinsically incompatible with achieving corporate objectives, then they would indeed be something to be avoided.

Once again, however, the valid criticism applies not to takeovers as such, but only to those takeovers which are not justified even on straightforward business grounds ... which represents a regrettably large number of the total. Business takeovers undertaken just to prevent management boredom[10], or to satisfy managements' imperial ambitions, or to follow commercial fashion, are indeed unethical. By diverting resources from proper business ends, such takeovers often cause enormous damage both to owner value and to stakeholders' lives. Since their objective is other than maximising long-term owner value[11], however, such takeovers are also strictly unbusinesslike; they violate not only ethical principles, but the financial ones underlying standard takeover theory. Such unbusinesslike takeovers are rightly to be deplored, and the managements who initiate them should be removed by the shareholders of the corporations whose resources they so egregiously waste.

What about the corporations that are the targets of bids, or who fear they might be? Isn't it unethical that their resources should have to be diverted to dealing with such threats? Not necessarily. However unfortunate it may seem that attention has to be paid to an unsolicited and unwelcome development, change is an inescapable part of life. Furthermore, even a bid that is contrary to the interests of the bidder may, either despite that fact – or sometimes precisely because of it – be in the best interests of the target: when an ambitious buyer is willing to pay over the odds, willing sellers can profit.

Each bid must be examined on its merits, from the point of view of the target as well as the bidder. Some bids are in the best

---

10   See, e.g., Bryan Burrough and John Helyar, *Barbarians at the Gate: The Fall of RJR Nabisco*, Harper & Row, 1990, p. 28 *inter alia*.

11   According to a survey of European companies conducted by KPMG, only 2 per cent of companies undertaking mergers or acquisitions cited increasing shareholder value as their reason for doing so. KPMG, *Colouring the Map*, cited in Jackson, Tony, 'Winning minds, not hearts', *Financial Times*, 27 October 1997, p. 14.

interests of all concerned. When, for example, the bidder is better run than the target, the target will typically benefit, ethically as well as economically, from the bidder's attentions; they force it to consider and improve its former ways. Those bids which are ill-judged, trivial or initiated mainly for their nuisance value are indeed unfortunate, and may seem like extortion to their targets. But such bids are also, by their very nature, likely to be counterproductive for the bidders initiating them. To the extent that takeovers have to be approved by shareholders (at least in well-ordered jurisdictions[12]), corporations that have genuinely achieved their owners' objectives are likely to be protected against such bids: they are less obvious targets, and are better able to defend themselves.

Hostile takeovers

But perhaps it is not takeovers generally, but hostile takeovers which are unethical. Once again, the answer is No, not necessarily; the key to the moral evaluation of hostile takeovers is understanding exactly what hostile takeovers are. Takeovers are not labelled 'hostile' because they are inimical to the interests of stakeholders. Nor are they called 'hostile' because they are intrinsically damaging. What renders a takeover hostile is simply opposition – for whatever reason – from the board of the target corporation: if the board does not welcome the bid, then the bid is considered

---

12   Which some US states, e.g. Delaware, are not. Consider the decision of the Delaware courts to uphold poison pills adopted without shareholder approval (Moran vs. Household Intl, 1985) and to overrule the wishes of Time's shareholders re the company's acquisition by Warner. See Robert A. G. Monks and Nell Minnow, *Power and Accountability* ('*PA*'), HarperCollins, 1991, p. 49, pp. 93–4.

hostile. Since, however, (UK) boards are normally dominated by executive directors, hostile takeovers are typically just those take-overs to which the *managers* of the target are hostile.

Managers have all sorts of reasons for opposing bids. They may be trying to provoke a higher offer price, and thus acting in the best interests of shareholders. Or they may be protecting their own vested interests: if the corporation is taken over, their very jobs are likely to be at stake. Each takeover must be examined on its individual merits, and be judged ethical according to whether it observes distributive justice and ordinary decency while pursuing the corporate objectives. The moral status of hostile takeovers is no different from that of other takeovers.

Why then are hostile takeovers so widely reviled? Mainly for the wrong reasons. It is not a legitimate criticism of business corporation X that it does not take as its objective the interests of an unrelated business corporation Y. Yet that is what is asserted when bidders, in such contexts normally called 'predators', are charged with not preserving or protecting the interests of their targets, often referred to as the 'prey'. It is not even the function of business X to maximise the long-term owner value of business Y. What X's objective should be, is simply to maximise the long-term owner value of X.[13]

That is not to say that hostile takeovers are never the occasion for immoral activity. Fierce contests with high stakes often provoke deplorable conduct, and contested bids are no exception. Given the different interests which are involved – predators and targets, managers and boards and owners, minority and majority shareholders – the likelihood of conflict is great, and the potential

---

13 Though once X takes over Y, maximising the long-term owner value of Y as part of the combined enterprise is the legitimate business of X.

for abuse of power is enormous. So some of the criticism of hostile takeovers is justified. But most of it is not.

In summary, it is not a valid criticism of traditional Anglo-American corporate governance that it allows takeovers: there is nothing immoral in takeovers as such. The genuine defect that is revealed by the examination of takeovers, is that the traditional system allows managers to pursue takeovers without adequate reference to the shareholders' objectives.

'Short-termism' encouraged[14]

But there is another criticism associated with takeovers that has to be considered. Doesn't the need to keep share prices up contribute to unethical 'short-termism'? Shareholders' short-sighted demands for dividends and for constant improvement in company profits are, it is often alleged, responsible for undermining long-term investment and planning. Instead of supporting British industry, shareholders 'disloyally' desert corporations for better returns elsewhere, and 'treacherously' accept takeover bids. Like so many popular criticisms, however, 'short-termism' in fact conceals a great many confused notions. Sometimes it is used as shorthand for the more fundamental complaint that British business is insufficiently productive or competitive or innovative. And sometimes it masks the converse fear, that British business is too innovative, all too ready opportunistically to desert traditional manufacturing for growth in the service sector.

---

14   This section draws heavily on Sternberg, *JB, op. cit.*, pp. 202–6.

However widespread they are, these criticisms are misguided.[15] Major research studies have shown that it is typically not shareholders, but industrial managers, whose perspective is excessively short-term.[16] According to these studies, industrial managers tend to evaluate projects on the basis of brief payback periods and the short-term profits that typically determine their own remuneration. Investment analysts, in contrast, tend to judge a company's performance on the basis of long-term sustainable cash flows … despite the fact that fund managers may be employed on short-term contracts.

A further study[17] has indeed calculated that despite the short-term objectives popularly associated with fund managers, the typical share holding period of large UK institutional investors is 18 years … long term by most human standards. That evaluation was further reinforced by a survey of senior directors of FTSE 100 companies, which discovered that fully 98 per cent considered their major shareholders to be long-term investors, and only 7 per cent felt hampered in adopting long-term strategies[18].

The flaw which would rightly be criticised as 'short-termism' is using an inappropriately short-term measure for evaluating

15   See Davies, 'Short-termism', *op. cit.*; Tim Congdon, 'How Britain Benefits from Short-termism' in *Stakeholding and its Critics*, Institute of Economic Affairs Health and Welfare Unit, 1997, pp. 19–36; Paul Marsh, 'Myths surrounding short-termism', *Financial Times Mastering Finance Supplement 6*, 16 June 1997.

16   See Paul Marsh, *Short-termism on Trial*, Institutional Fund Managers' Association, 1990, and Gareth Stainer, *Shareholder Value Analysis Survey*, Coopers & Lybrand Deloitte, 1991.

17   By World Markets, reported in Barry Riley, 'Short-termism revisited and recalculated', *Financial Times*, 16 April 1997, p. 29.

18   April 1998 *Financial Times* journalist poll of mainly finance directors, with a 74 per cent response rate; reported in Jane Martinson, 'Shares in the action' and 'Companies say big shareholders take a long view', *Financial Times*, 27 April 1998, pp. 21 and 1.

corporate performance. In business, for example, current period accounting profits are not necessarily a good gauge of long-term owner value; nor is return on capital employed when measured over too short a period.[19] If industry and investors – often otherwise known as managers and owners – are using different criteria, then it is hardly surprising that they are working at cross purposes. The solution is for both to use the same measure in pursuit of the same end: the definitive purpose of the corporation, which for business is maximising long-term owner value.

Nevertheless, institutions are still frequently exhorted to take a more 'responsible' attitude to their investments, to support the companies they invest in when things go wrong, not sell their shares … to be, in the American phrase, 'relationship investors'. However well-meant this injunction may be, it is nevertheless based on a confused understanding of the role of the shareholder and of the corporation. Loyalty does not require that shareholders stay with a company when its performance is deficient. It may sometimes be appropriate to allow a company time to recover, or to help it do so, but the relationship of shareholder to corporation is not that of friend or family member, social worker or doctor; shareholders do not have a Hippocratic duty to heal or preserve the corporation. Nor do corporations have any right to life. The notional perpetual life enjoyed by a corporation enables it to survive any particular group of mortal investors, but if the corporation no longer meets the requirements of its shareholders, it can legitimately be wound up.

To say that all shareholders should necessarily be long-term or

---

19   For an explanation of why such measures are an inadequate measure of long-term owner value, see Sternberg, *JB, op. cit.*, pp. 45–9.

active holders is to reverse the relationship of owner to property: if any fealty is owed, it is by the corporation to the shareholder, not *vice versa*. There is no moral obligation either to become, or to continue to be, a shareholder. Being a shareholder is only one of the myriad roles open to an individual or an institution, and the reasons for choosing to be a shareholder are correspondingly diverse. Equally, there is no moral obligation to be an active shareholder; shareholder activity is justified if and only if it helps to achieve the shareholder's objective in being a shareholder. This does not mean that while they own shares, shareholders have no obligations in respect of their holdings. Those obligations are, however, very limited: they consist mainly of using the corporate objective as their criterion for decisions concerning the conduct of the corporation.[20]

Though some objectives encourage long-term holdings and shareholder activism, others do not; they can, however, be equally legitimate reasons for owning shares. And it is the shareholder's objectives for owning shares which should determine if a particular holding is to be bought or sold, simply kept or actively managed: the long-term goals appropriate for a pension fund may well not be sensible for any given pensioner. Insofar as an individual's or institution's objective in owning shares is to maximise financial gain, the buy/hold/sell decision will turn on whether the proceeds obtainable from selling the shares are greater than the value expected from keeping them. If they are, the shareholder is *right* to sell.[21]

Nevertheless, shareholders are routinely criticised for doing

---

20 See *ibid.*, especially pp. 206–8.
21 Morally as well as economically.

so: their decisions to sell are castigated as somehow wrong, or irresponsible, especially if the sale is to a hostile bidder or a foreigner. What such charges imply, however, is that either the shareholder's calculation is inaccurate, or that the objective of financial maximisation is illegitimate. But if such financial maximisation is illegitimate, then so is all business .... What is ostensibly a criticism of the traditional Anglo-American corporate governance system, is actually an attack on business as such.

That the business objective is the real target is also clear in the other popular version of the 'short-termism' argument, which criticises Anglo-American business for concentrating on financial gain for shareholders rather than product excellence or customer satisfaction. Because they are so narrowly focused on short-term financial outcomes, the argument claims, Anglo-American firms invest too little, and thus sacrifice the excellence and innovation needed for long-term success. This argument is, however, fundamentally flawed.[22] Not only is it empirically dubious[23], but it relies on a conceptual misunderstanding of business and corporate governance.

Contrary to popular belief, the definitive objective of business is not maximising current period accounting profits; it is, instead, maximising long-term owner value. Owner value naturally reflects the distant, indirect and qualitative effects of current actions; it is automatically reduced by actions that undermine the business's ability to thrive over the long term. Accounting profits, in contrast,

---

22 For a closely related analysis, see 'The performance argument' in Chapter 6 below (pp. 139–40).

23 See Davies, 'Short-termism', *op. cit.;* Congdon, 'How Britain Benefits', *op. cit.*; Marsh, 'Myths surrounding short-termism', *op. cit.*; and Lucian Arye Bebchuk and Oren Bar-Gill, 'Misreporting Corporate Performance', Discussion Paper, November 2002; http://papers.ssrn.com/paper.taf?abstract_id=354141.

provide only a snapshot measure of performance; they can therefore be increased, at least temporarily, by actions whose long-term effects on value are negative.

When business is properly understood, satisfying customers is normally not opposed to business success, but is a condition of achieving it: businesses are most likely to survive and thrive when they provide customers with what they genuinely prize. Sacrificing long-term value for short-term benefits is bad business practice.[24] The activity of maximising owner value is both intrinsically long-term in its orientation, and perfectly compatible with the Anglo-American model of corporate governance. What critics of 'short-termism' should attack, therefore, is bad business practice, not the Anglo-American model of corporate governance.

But perhaps what the critics of 'short-termism' want is for firms to ignore owner value, and to commit themselves instead to the long-term pursuit of innovation or excellence or customer satisfaction as ends in themselves. If so, then their target is clearly the business objective: pursuing excellence at any cost may be a noble activity, but it is a different undertaking than doing business. Though there can be good reasons for sometimes preferring the activities of producing the very best widget (healthcare, education, newspaper) to business, there is no justification for confusing such activities with business. Whichever end is preferred, however, corporate governance is not at issue: what is in dispute is which objective should be pursued, not the methods of keeping corporations to the chosen objective.

---

24 So is subjugating long-term owner value to such supposedly long-term objectives as full employment or market share: consider the fate of the Japanese and other Asian economies.

'Excessive' remuneration allowed

Another confused charge that is frequently levelled against trad-itional Anglo-American corporate governance, is that it allows excessive executive remuneration. Though the amounts are com-monly described as 'obscene' and 'unethical', the basic assumption of excess is itself open to question. Once again, since the criticisms usually apply to business corporations, the examples used will be drawn from business.

What determines whether pay is excessive, is whether it is *deserved*. And it is deserved if it appropriately reflects real con-tributions to achieving the corporate objective. Unfortunately, both critics and defenders of top pay have overlooked this central importance of distributive justice, and have focused instead on emotive irrelevancies. Contrary to popular opinion, high pay is not unethical because it excites envy or satisfies greed; the 'going rate' and executive motivation are equally irrelevant to the moral defence of corporate rewards.

First, it is simply not true that large pay differentials are nec-essarily unethical, however much such assertions may appeal to the sentimental and the resentful. Claims that pay differentials are immoral often rely on the notion that there is a natural 'just wage', applicable everywhere and always. That mistaken view in turn usually reflects another misguided belief, that corporate re-muneration is a measure of human dignity, or a reward for moral character.

Properly understood, however, corporate remuneration is simply a payment for services rendered. What determines what those services are worth to a corporation, and accordingly how much it should pay for them, is the contribution that the services make to achieving the corporate objective. That in turn depends on both the quality of the employee's actual performance and the firm's specific circumstances. For a shirker, £5000 a year can be too much pay; £5 million may be too little for an innovator who has added many times that amount to the value of a business corporation.

Widening differentials in pay often reflect widening differentials in the contributions made to achieving the corporate objective. When they do, they are justified ethically as well as economically. High pay rises can even be perfectly compatible with redundancies. When traditional functions are no longer useful, and managing change requires increasingly sophisticated management skills, it will be right to pay top executives more while shedding unnecessary staff.

Another common mistake is the notion that high pay is immoral because it rewards executive greed. Employees' motives affect the morality of corporate remuneration only insofar as they affect the achievement of the corporate objective. Accordingly, the fact that corporate executives are often motivated by things other than money – by intrinsic interest in the job, by the wish to provide for their families, and, more dangerously, by lust for power[25] – also has no bearing on what constitutes just remuneration.

References to the 'going rate' are equally irrelevant. The 'going rate' is simply the market price of a category of employee. Whether or not it should be paid requires comparing that price with the contributions to the corporate objective expected from

---

25   According to a study of 400 'high-flyers' in 200 companies, only 2 per cent said they were motivated by money, whereas nearly 40 per cent sought to achieve senior rank. Roffley Park Management Institute, *High-Flyers and Succession Planning in Changing Organisations*; cited in Lucy Kellaway, 'Onwards and alongwards', *Financial Times*, 23 April 1998, p. 21.

the employee. Unless the contributions exceed the cost, paying it will not be justified – ethically or financially.

Sadly, that fundamental principle has been missed not just by critics of high pay, but by its defenders. Executive remuneration cannot be justified by the fact that it represents only a small part of total corporate expenditure. Although when compared with turnover, pay is often immaterial, this does not mean that it is necessarily merited. And if profits are the basis for judging materiality, then *any* positive remuneration will be ruled out when a corporation is losing money. What makes business remuneration ethical is not how it compares with sales or current period accounting profits, or how much it leaves over to pay other workers, but whether it properly reflects the employee's contribution to owner value.

And on that basis, sadly, some executive pay is indefensible. The business executive whose remuneration increases while the value of the company he manages declines, is indeed being rewarded unfairly. Some of the discrepancies arise from time-lagged remuneration, and the exercise of (irrevocable, unconditional, one way and often subsequently adjusted) options awarded in palmier times. All too often, however, the measures used even for performance-related pay are simply too 'loser friendly', being awarded by executives to executives without reference to the corporate objectives.[26]

In summary, what is properly criticised is not high executive pay as such, or pay that is 'excessive' on ideological grounds unrelated to corporate performance. The appropriate target for criticism is a system that makes executive pay – and indeed all

---

26 For a review of other corporate governance problems that relate to remuneration, see Chapter 4 below.

corporate remuneration – insufficiently responsive to achieving the corporate purposes. What is needed is not regulatory control of executive excesses, but shareholder supervision of corporate remuneration policies. To the extent that particular implementations of Anglo-American corporate governance impede shareholder supervision, it is those practices, not the theory, that need changing.

Auditors' inadequacies

Another subject beset by confusion is the role of the auditor. One of the main reasons for convening the UK Cadbury Committee on the Financial Aspects of Corporate Governance in 1992 was that a disturbing number of large firms had gone bankrupt or fallen prey to fraud with little or no apparent warning. Believing that auditors should have been able to detect signs of the impending disasters, commentators called for better corporate governance as a remedy. But although there is undoubtedly cause for concern when major corporations and vast sums of money disappear, auditors play at most a peripheral role in corporate governance.[27] The faults that have been attributed to auditors have usually been those of the managements[28], the directors or the shareholders themselves.

It is inappropriate to expect financial auditors to detect most sorts of fraud and operational problems, because that is not their job. As Lord Justice Lopes famously remarked: 'An auditor is not bound to be a detective, or as it was said, to approach his work

---

27   For a discussion of the moral hazard created by requiring financial audits, see Chapter 7 below.

28   See, e.g., Bebchuk and Bar-Gill, 'Misreporting Corporate Performance', *op. cit.*.

with suspicion or with a foregone conclusion that there is something wrong. He is a watchdog, but not a bloodhound.'[29].

A financial audit is rather like a Ministry of Transport car inspection. The MOT only checks whether a vehicle can pass a few functional tests; it examines the brakes, the tyres and the lights. The MOT does not guarantee that the vehicle is safe or that it is good value. In like fashion, an auditor merely confirms that financial statements have been drawn up in accordance with Generally Accepted Accounting Principles. Financial auditors do not determine which of the many perfectly legal variants allowed by those principles should be employed; far less do they guarantee the general health or viability of the underlying business.[30] Blaming auditors for not detecting impending corporate failures is as inappropriate as blaming MOT inspectors for not predicting when a car will run out of petrol.

The belief that auditors are to blame for not predicting corporate failures stems largely from the 'expectation gap' that exists between what the auditor's role actually is and what it is popularly thought to be. The auditor's duty is indeed to certify whether the financial accounts present *a* 'true and fair' picture of corporate operations. Fulfilling that duty, however, does not require[31] auditors

29 In re Kingston Cotton Mills Co. (1896) 2 Ch 279.

30 UK auditors have been advised to state explicitly that they are not expressing an opinion on the ability of London Stock Exchange listed companies to continue as going concerns (Auditing Practices Board Bulletin 1996/3 *Disclosures Relating to Corporate Governance (Supplement)*, para. 19). And the US *Statement on Auditing Standards* No. 59 para. 04 states: 'The auditor is not responsible for predicting future conditions or events'.

31 Exceptionally, the auditors of UK financial institutions are now required to report irregularities to the regulators (SAS 620), and the auditors of UK pension funds are bound by Section 48(1) of the Pensions Act 1995 immediately to report in writing to the Occupational Pensions Regulatory Authority if they have 'reasonable cause' to suspect any material irregularities in the administration

to be general purpose detectives. As interpreted by regulators and auditors' professional associations, the auditor's responsibility is largely formal, and is satisfied by pronouncing on the technical ways in which financial accounts are drawn up. Shareholders' objectives might well be better served by a more substantial assessment of corporate operations against the constitutional corporate objectives; an outline of what a 'governance audit' might involve is provided in Chapter 8 below. But it is not currently the responsibility of financial auditors to evaluate anything but the choice and application of accounting procedures.

Once the extremely limited role of the financial audit is understood, the conflicts of interest that are frequently thought to undermine auditors' independence become less significant as corporate governance flaws. It is appropriate for auditors to be appointed by and report directly to the board rather than management, and not to audit their own work. But since it is not the auditor's responsibility to detect fraud or deviations from corporate policy, it is less important that auditors' independence of judgement might be compromised by the lucrative non-auditing assignments that their firms might hope to obtain from the corporation's management, or by pricing audits as loss leaders.[32] The corporate governance role that is mistakenly attributed to financial auditors is actually the responsibility of the directors.

---

of a pension scheme. Even this latter explicit 'whistle-blowing' duty, however, does not require the auditor to look for such irregularities. It is noteworthy that although Article 307 of the (US) Sarbanes-Oxley Act 2002 imposes an 'up the ladder' reporting duty on attorneys who suspect material violations of securities law or of fiduciary responsibility, it places no such obligation on auditors.

32   It is noteworthy that neither were problems for Enron.

Obstacle to efficient performance

That essential supervisory function has itself been the subject of much criticism. So has corporate governance itself, for interfering with efficient corporate performance. Unfortunately, the charge is sometimes justified. When corporate governance is mistakenly equated with imposing 'social responsibilities' not endorsed by the shareholders, then challenges in the name of corporate governance will indeed impede proper corporate functioning. Equally, when corporate governance is wrongly identified with 'hygiene' specifications that rigidly limit executive remuneration or require stipulated numbers of non-executive directors, it often reflects popular ideology rather than shareholders' genuine interests. And when members of the board represent factional interests, or shareholder votes are unrelated to the corporate purposes, they, too, are likely to be obstructive. Finally, when corporate governance measures are enacted through regulation, they are bound to be inflexible and intrusive. In all these cases, however, the culprit is neither corporate governance as such, nor the Anglo-American model of corporate governance: culpability lies instead with activities that are inimical to good corporate governance properly understood.

When corporate governance refers to shareholder-approved, structural methods of ensuring that a corporation's actions are directed at the definitive corporate purpose, what is objectionable is not corporate governance but objections to it. It is notable that those who claim that active corporate governance interferes with corporate functioning are usually senior corporate executives. In evaluating their claim, it is essential to remember that a key purpose of corporate governance is precisely to prevent managers from pursuing their own interests in place of the shareholders' interests. When managers perceive corporate governance as interference, it may well be a sign that the managers are pursuing the wrong objectives; if they are, then interference is right and proper. A similar argument applies to charges that having non-executives on the board is 'divisive'. It is better to have at least one division of the board championing the interests of the shareholders, than to have a board that is united against the shareholders' interests.

A genuine problem would exist if corporations' legitimate activities were hindered by corporate governance-inspired attempts to monitor them. As opponents of corporate governance often point out, uprooting plants to check their progress is hardly the best way to foster vegetative growth. But even when that analogy does apply, the culprit is not corporate governance, but bad judgement. Because the purpose of corporate governance is to promote achievement of the corporate objective, the amount and type of monitoring must be consistent with that purpose; monitoring that undermines achievement of the corporate purpose is self-defeating. The way to prevent non-constructive interference is not to ignore corporate governance, but to ensure that all those charged with performing it are both competent, and motivated, to do it properly.

Lack of 'shareholder democracy'

Another misguided criticism levelled against the traditional Anglo-American system of corporate governance, is that it is inimical to 'shareholder democracy'. The slogan 'shareholder democracy' has historically referred to the (British) Conservative Party's aim of making more of the electorate into shareholders, chiefly by encouraging them to purchase shares in privatisation offerings. The phrase has, however, also been used to designate the quite different notion that corporations should be democratically controlled, either by their shareholders[33] or sometimes by the electorate as a whole[34].

Charges of a lack of 'shareholder democracy' have typically emerged when small shareholders have been unsuccessful in opposing corporate policies, notably executive remuneration schemes in the privatised industries. What such charges reveal, however, is not any defect of the traditional methods of corporate governance, but a misunderstanding of what 'shareholder democracy' entails.

Democracy means something very different in corporations than it does in government. Whereas the principle of democracy in government is 'one man, one vote', the corresponding principle in a corporation[35] is 'one *share*, one vote'. Since the right to control the corporation stems from ownership of the corporation, voting rights are normally proportional to the percentage of corporate capital that is owned. The equality that exists in corporate elections is not the notional equality of moral agents, or equality under the law, but the equality of fungible shares of capital[36].

When it is understood that votes attach to shares, not heads, it can be seen that the outrage expressed by frustrated investors

33 The concept of majority rule in corporate elections has long been recognised in English law.

34 In which form it is sometimes known as 'stakeholder democracy'.

35 Limited by shares.

36 Of the same class; different types of shares may legitimately enjoy different voting rights. Even in the UK, where the principle of 'one share, one vote' is normally respected, common shares typically enjoy greater voting rights than preference shares, and the UK government's 'Golden Share' in privatisations has an overriding veto. It should be noted that proposals to counter 'short-termism' by conferring extra votes on shares held for more than a stipulated period (as in France, where shares held for more than four years acquire double voting rights) clearly violate this fundamental principle of corporate democracy.

is generally misplaced. The inability of individual shareholders to get their views implemented is not an indication that shareholder democracy is absent. It is, instead, direct evidence of democracy in action. The reason why the views of individual shareholders seldom prevail is simply because in most major jurisdictions, individual investors own only a small fraction of the outstanding shares.

What the thwarted small shareholders are experiencing is in fact one of the most fundamental features of democracy: the 'tyranny of the majority'[37]. The oddity is not that it is occurs in corporate elections, but that the same people who so strenuously object to it there, seem oblivious to its operation elsewhere. It may be that expectations of control are greater in respect of property than of government, or that the lack of control is more obvious in the smaller corporate arena. Or it may be that people are more sensitive to their rights as owners than to their liberties as citizens. Whatever the reason, however, share ownership rights do not include the right automatically to prevail.[38] It is neither surprising nor undemocratic that ownership of a (typically small) part does not normally confer control of the whole. Nor is it inappropriate that more than a simple majority should be needed to make constitutional changes.

37 See Alexis de Tocqueville, *Democracy in America*, 1835, Volume I, Chapter 15, 'On the Omnipotence of the Majority in the United States and its Effects'.

38 In both the corporate and the political arena, minority interests can have disproportionate influence when they represent the marginal votes necessary to get first-past-the-post, especially when voter apathy means that pluralities are not majorities. When that happens, however, the majority of those voting still wins. Insofar as more-than-50-per-cent majorities are required for, e.g., changes in ownership structures, shareholders with relatively small holdings can in fact have even greater influence, and exercise what is sometimes called 'negative control'.

Once again, the real target is not the mechanism, but the outcomes it allows. This is shown by the fact that devices proposed as ways of increasing shareholder democracy – reserving seats on the board for small shareholders[39], for example – would in fact reduce it in order to give small shareholders disproportionate power. The notion that an elected representative's function is to represent the special interests of his particular electors, rather than the electorate as a whole, is itself a debatable, though increasingly common, view of democratic representation. It is, moreover, incompatible with the principle that decision-making for the corporation should be determined by the purpose of the corporation.

While they are shareholders, each shareholder should make the distinguishing purpose of the corporation the basis for his/its decisions concerning the conduct of the corporation.[40] Reference to the corporate purpose is crucial: without agreement on a common objective, common ownership founders in even the simplest matters.[41] If all shareholders independently use achieving the corporate objective as their decision criterion, they will not necessarily agree about what is right, but they will at least understand what is relevant.

---

39 See Andrew Hill, 'A rattle grows louder at Italy's boardroom doors', *Financial Times*, 24 June 1996, p. 19; Global News Wire – Asia Africa Intelligence Wire, *Business Line* (India), 24 February 2003, 'Small Shareholders on Company Boards May be Mandatory' (online; no page number given).

40 As argued in Sternberg, *JB* (*op. cit.*, pp. 202–4), paying due regard to the corporate purpose is the essence of being a responsible shareholder. A responsible shareholder who wants to change the purpose of the corporation, or to use some principle other than the current corporate end as the basis for his decisions concerning the corporation, will make that fact explicit.

41 Consider what is likely to happen when one joint-purchaser of a motorcar plans to maintain it as a classic museum piece, but the other wants to use it as a family runabout ... the outcome is unlikely to be happy motoring.

In summary, then, the Anglo-American model of corporate governance is not necessarily inimical to shareholder democracy or to corporate performance. It has no necessary connection with damaging short-termism or particular vulnerability to auditors' inadequacies. And it is none the worse morally for allowing takeovers and high remuneration.

4 COMMON CRITICISMS: GENUINE

Although the criticisms considered in Chapter 3 are spurious, many others levelled against the traditional Anglo-American system of corporate governance unfortunately are not. Considered as a way of keeping corporate directors accountable to corporate owners, and of keeping corporate actions tied to the corporate purpose, the practice in many Anglo-American jurisdictions often does fall seriously short of the traditional theory. It does so in three main ways. General meetings and corporate elections do not enable shareholders adequately to control corporate direction. Directors are often ill-equipped to exercise their fiduciary duties, insufficiently accountable to shareholders, and insufficiently independent of management. And institutional investors are insufficiently accountable to the ultimate beneficial owners of the funds they manage.

These are severe defects, which have been increasingly recognised. No attempt will be made here, however, to assess the comparative frequency of the different classes of defects, or the damage they have done. Nor will there be any attempt to assign blame for these defects. Rather, given the conceptual objectives of *Corporate Governance: Accountability in the Marketplace*, this chapter will simply indicate some of the ways in which the defects hinder proper corporate governance, with a view to indicating possible corrections in Chapter 8 below.

Democratic deficits

The ability of shareholders to control corporate direction is severely limited by the procedures which govern general meetings and corporate elections. So serious is the problem that, according to the Report of a City/Industry Working Group, the Annual General Meeting as constituted in Britain is 'an expensive waste of time and money'[1]. Equally, it has been said that American corporate elections are 'procedurally much more akin to the elections held by the Communist Party of North Korea than those held in Western democracies'.[2] How can this be so?

First, the agenda of general meetings is set by the directors, not the shareholders. As pollsters and politicians know well, the way in which questions are phrased can do much to influence the answers; directors' ability to propose and to word resolutions significantly limits shareholder powers. One standard ploy, for example, is to combine conceptually distinct matters in a single resolution.[3] When, for example, the only way in which shareholders can oppose a particular board policy is to oppose re-election of the directors, shareholders' ability to control the strategic direction of their

---

1   Reported in *Shareholder Communications at the Annual General Meeting: A Consultative Document*, Department of Trade and Industry, April 1996 (henceforth 'DTI'), para. 1.11, p. 5.

2   Edward Jay Epstein, *Who Owns the Corporation? Management vs. Shareholders*, Priority Press, New York, 1986, p. 13, quoted in Monks and Minnow, *PA*, *op. cit.*, online version at http://www.lens-inc.com/power/power.htm, Chapter 7, para. 77. See also a March 1994 editorial co-authored by former SEC Commissioner Philip Lochner and CalPERS General Council Richard Koppes, which condemned traditional US annual meetings as an 'empty ritual' and a 'monumental waste of time and energy'; reported in John C. Wilcox, 'Rethinking the Annual Meeting', Georgeson Report; ftp://georgeson.com/pub/greport/meeting.txt.

3   Note that Clause 2.2 of the UK Combined Code recommends a separate resolution for each 'substantially separate issue'.

companies is significantly reduced. Even when resolutions on a given topic are presented to the shareholders, their votes may be advisory only.[4]

Depending on the jurisdiction, it is either difficult or impossible for shareholders to get binding resolutions of their own on to the agenda. To be considered by the board, shareholder resolutions must usually be backed by material percentages of voting shares; in some jurisdictions, those shares must also have been held for qualifying periods.[5] In the UK, there is no standard procedure for getting a resolution on to an extraordinary general meeting ('EGM') agenda; the methods provided for annual general meetings ('AGMs') do not apply. Even when shareholders are permitted to propose resolutions, they may be seriously inhibited from doing so by the fear of personally having to bear the costs of circulating them to all shareholders.[6] Finally, the subject matter permitted for shareholder resolutions is often severely limited. In the US, regulation precludes shareholder resolutions concerning

---

4   Consider directors' remuneration. Schedule 7A of the (UK) Companies Act 1985 (as amended by the Directors' Remuneration Report Regulations (SI 2002/1986 – DRRR)) specifies the contents of a remuneration report which must be approved by the board and presented to the shareholders for approval. The shareholders' vote is advisory only, however, and merely serves to register shareholder opinion.

5   In the UK, for example, resolutions must be proposed by shareholders representing at least 5 per cent of the voting rights or by at least 100 shareholders with shares on which at least £100 on average has been paid up (Companies Act 1985, Section 376). In the US, companies need only consider resolutions when their holders own a minimum of 1 per cent of the securities entitled to vote on the proposition, or own shares with a market value of $2,000, and the shares must have been held for at least one year. SEC Reg. §240 14a-8(b)(1).

6   Currently under review in the UK; *DTI, op. cit.*.

'the conduct of the ordinary business operations'[7] of the company or company elections[8]; nor usually can shareholder resolutions bind the board[9], even when passed unanimously[10]. Under Delaware law, shareholders cannot initiate charter amendments or proposals to merge, sell, or dissolve their corporations; they do not even have veto power over dividend decisions.[11]

Should a shareholder resolution succeed in getting on to the agenda, its chances of being approved are reduced by the procedures for conducting corporate elections. In the US, severe restrictions still apply to proxy contests, even though SEC pre-clearance is no longer required for all communications to shareholders. The beneficial owners of UK shares held through nominee accounts still have no right either to receive corporate information, or to attend General Meetings; proxies may not be used to vote in a show of hands or even to raise questions.[12] Furthermore, when voting is not confidential, the managements counting the votes know

---

7   SEC Reg §240.14a-8 (17 CFR 240.14a-8(c)(7)). This restriction has, however, started to be relaxed with the 1998 reversal of the Cracker Barrel no-action letter on employment-related proposals raising social policy issues. Securities and Exchange Commission 17 CFR Part 240 Release No. 34-40018; IC-23200; File No. S7-25-97.

8   SEC Reg §240.14a-8(i)8.

9   Directors are free to disregard precatory shareholder resolutions that take place under the securities law. See Speigel vs. Buntrock, 571 A. 2d 767, 775-76 (Del. 1990), quoted in Lucian Arye Bebchuk, 'The Case for Empowering Shareholders', April 2003, p. 9, http://papers.ssrn.com/paper.taf?abstract_id=387940.

10   Binding resolutions are presumed not to be a proper subject of shareholder action under state law (excludable under SEC Reg.§240.14a-8(i)1) and/or to preclude the board's ability to exercise business judgement, thus usurping its fiduciary role (and excludable under SEC Reg §240. 14a-8(i)7, 'Management functions'). To circumvent this restriction, precatory language is usually employed.

11   Bebchuk, "The Case for Empowering Shareholders", *op. cit.*, pp. 10–12.

12   At the meetings of public companies unless the articles of the company so provide; see section 372, Companies Act 1985.

how shareholders have voted, and can use their corporate power to impose commercial sanctions against those who vote against them.[13] Because voting imposes such high direct and opportunity costs on shareholders, voting levels in UK company elections remain less than the DTI target of 60 per cent.[14] Corporate elections, which in theory should do much to keep shareholders in control of their property, are thus significantly less effective in practice.[15]

Directors' defects

The obstacles to accountability go beyond the procedural defects of corporate elections; they extend as well to the conduct of directors. Directors often lack both the qualities and the resources they need to protect shareholders' interests; they are insufficiently independent of management, and insufficiently accountable to shareholders.

13 By, for example, not awarding pension fund management or insurance or banking business to their opponents. From mid 2003, investment companies and investment advisers registered in the US will be required by the SEC to have and to disclose their proxy voting policies and procedures as well as their actual votes. Securities and Exchange Commission 17 CFR Parts 239, 249, 270, and 274, Release Nos. 33-8188, 34-47304, IC-25922; File No. S7-36-02.

14 Overall 2002 turnout rates increased to 55.86 per cent from 52.72 per cent in 2001; average turnout at FTSE 100 company meetings was 49 per cent. (Manifest Information Services Ltd, *Proxy Poll Data 2002, An analysis of proxy voting trends at UK shareholder meetings*, Table 5, http://www.manifest.co.uk/reports/proxypoll2002.html). Cf. the under 40 per cent level reported by the Hampel Committee on Corporate Governance (*Preliminary Report*, August 1997, para. 5.7.).

15 Responding to an August 2002 petition (File No. 4-461), the SEC is undertaking a comprehensive review of shareholder proposals, director elections, proxy solicitations, shareholder takeovers of boards through proxy fights, and disclosure requirements imposed on large shareholders and groups of investors. See www.corporategovernance.com.

The most fundamental obstacle to directors' performing their essential role, is a simple failure to understand the nature of that role. Too often, directors have been regarded – by themselves and by those who appoint them – as nothing more than senior sorts of managers. The directors' central obligation – their fiduciary duty to protect the shareholders' interests[16] – is insufficiently recognised.

Because the directorial role is not adequately understood, little is done to ensure that directors have either the personal qualities or the practical resources they need to perform their specifically directorial duties. Judging from the selection procedures that are still widely used, directors are often appointed because they have influential contacts or specific business experience. While undoubtedly useful, those characteristics are, at best, only incidentally related to the intelligence, judgement and moral courage that are the essential directorial qualities. Directors must be able to identify the key issues confronting the corporation; they must be able to ask the questions that are necessary to safeguard the owners' interests; and they must be able to obtain and evaluate and act on the answers.

Performing such critical functions is particularly difficult when the directors of a corporation are also its executives: it is notoriously difficult even to recognise, far less to criticise and correct, one's own mistakes or those of one's close colleagues. Executive directors' interests as managers often differ significantly from those of the shareholders they are meant to protect; executive directors may well have a vested interest in defending an unsatisfactory *status quo*. The same conflict of interest that makes corporate

---

16 In some jurisdictions, the directors' duty is technically to protect the interests of the corporation. Since, however, its interests can only be defined by reference to the objectives given to it by the shareholders, the interests of the corporation are conceptually the same as the shareholders' interests as defined here.

governance necessary can arise within the individuals charged with providing it.

One remedy increasingly suggested to reduce this fundamental conflict of interest is to have non-executive directors, sometimes called 'external directors' or 'independent directors'.[17] Not being managers of the corporation, non-executives may find it easier to challenge the actions of management should it be necessary. But even genuinely independent non-executives are not immune to conflicts of interest[18]: the non-executives of one corporation are often executives of some other, and may be protective of the interests that all managements have in common. Individuals who are directors of more than one corporation may indeed be subject to a positive conflict of obligation.[19]

Independence does, in any case, require more than not being an executive.[20] Although in theory all directors are equal, it can be difficult for non-executive and less senior executive directors to challenge autocratic or charismatic leaders, or to insist on raising topics not on the agenda set by the chairman.[21] Furthermore, performing the specifically directorial duties often requires more time than directors have, either at board meetings or in prepara-

---

17 Consider, for example, the Higgs Report, *op. cit.*.

18 Which do not necessarily lead to immoral or inappropriate conduct; see Sternberg, *JB*, *op. cit.*, especially pp. 100–2.

19 See *ibid.*, pp. 101–2.

20 According to the Higgs Report, 'A non-executive director is considered independent when the board determines that the director is independent in character and judgement, and there are no relationships or circumstances which could affect, or appear to affect, the director's judgement' (A.3.4).

21 Unless the individual has the requisite character and skills, complying with the Higgs Report recommendation to appoint a Senior Independent Director will simply add to company bureaucracy and expense.

tion for them: non-executives are usually part-time, and executives are preoccupied with their demanding executive jobs. Although these issues have been addressed by the Higgs Report, its reference to perceived as well as actual obstacles to independence, and inclusion of questionable criteria of independence[22] suggests that its implementation is as likely to exclude valuable candidates as to prevent damaging conflicts.

For directors to perform their fiduciary duties properly, they also need information and expertise that is independent of the company's management. But it is seldom available. Board papers advising directors are normally prepared by corporate executives with distinct departmental interests. Executive directors are often ill-informed about areas outside their functional responsibilities, while non-executives typically lack any independent access to company information or the company's staff; they may personally have to bear any expenses they incur in investigating company matters.

Directors' accountability to the shareholders is also impaired by the ways in which directors are selected, appointed, and remunerated. In the US, most non-executive directors are nominated by the chief executive; shareholders are effectively barred by SEC regulation from nominating directors. In the UK, shareholders may nominate directors, but most nominations are still made by boards themselves. Unfortunately, directors whose nominations depend on the board can be reluctant actively to monitor those who were responsible for their selection. Even wholly non-executive nomination committees can be insufficient

---

22   E.g., long experience of being a director is deemed an impediment to being an independent director of that same company.

to protect directorial independence when cross-directorships are commonplace.

The effectiveness of directors as corporate governors is also jeopardised by the way in which they are remunerated. A remuneration committee composed solely of non-executives can help to keep executive directors from directly setting their own rewards. But the fact that the non-executives of one corporation are typically the executives of another may still limit their willingness to curb executive pay; even the 'independent experts' they consult are normally themselves executives who are hired and paid by other executives. Directorial functions are seldom evaluated and remunerated separately from executive responsibilities.

An even more fundamental obstacle to directors' effectiveness comes from the form of payment. Because option schemes give a one-way bet, they are as likely to cause directors' interests to diverge from, as to coincide with, shareholders' interests.[23] Directors whose pay is guaranteed through long-term rolling contracts may be prohibitively expensive to dismiss[24]; the holders of 'golden parachutes' enjoy effective immunity even against takeovers. Ironically, the best and most direct way of aligning directors' interests with those of shareholders – by paying them with shares – is routinely rejected by groups ostensibly defend-

---

23 'No owner has ever escaped the burden of capital costs, whereas a holder of a fixed-price option bears no capital costs at all. An owner must weigh upside potential against downside risk; an option holder has no downside.' Warren Buffet, Berkshire Hathaway, Inc., *Annual Report to Shareholders*, 1985, p. 12; quoted in Monks and Minnow, *PA, op. cit.*, p. 173.

24 In 2002, only 62 per cent of FTSE 350 companies had all of their executives on contracts of one year or less, up from 40 per cent in 1999. Tony Tassell, 'Most top companies miss best practice standards', *Financial Times*, 25 April 2003, p. 2. See also note 28 below.

ing shareholders' interests.[25] And although performance-related pay is intended to ensure that directors advance shareholders' interests, it is frequently so badly designed that it does precisely the reverse.

Badly designed performance-related remuneration schemes often constitute a significant moral hazard[26]: they provide a positive incentive for directors (and other corporate agents) to undermine the interests of shareholders. The specific performances to which the remuneration is related may themselves be harmful to shareholders' interests. When, for example, additions to sales or total assets are rewarded without regard to costs, large loss-making operations are a natural result. And unless the performance-related scheme takes into account risks as well as rewards, directors will be positively encouraged to gamble recklessly with the company's future.

There are few if any sanctions available to shareholders when directors fail to perform their essential role. Although most directors do now have to stand for re-election[27], significant numbers of directors are still elected for periods of two years or

---

25 Consider the recommendations of such organisations as the (UK) Institutional Shareholders Committee ('ISC'; *The Role and Duties of Directors – A Statement of Best Practice*, August 1993) and PRO NED (*Remuneration Committees*, p. 11). See also, for example, the Institute of Directors' ('IoD'), Institute of Chartered Secretaries and Administrators' ('ICSA'), and The Association of Corporate Treasurers' ('ACT') responses to the Higgs consultation.

26 See Sternberg, *JB, op. cit.*, especially pp. 103–4, 152–4.

27 As recently as 1996, 10 per cent of the UK's largest 300 companies by market capitalisation failed to require their directors to stand for re-election, according to National Association of Pension Funds estimates. William Lewis, 'Institutions press for all directors to face re-election', *Financial Times*, 25 September 1996, p. 1.

longer.[28] Directors who are appointed for long fixed terms are largely protected from shareholder disapproval. Legal sanctions against directors are very expensive and of limited usefulness … especially in the US, where directors' duties of care and loyalty have been seriously eroded.[29] State legislation has limited directors' liability, even for gross negligence. It has also permitted directors to be indemnified against errors and omissions at shareholders' expense, even when the courts have found directors to be in breach of their duty. Shareholders challenging the actions of directors can therefore find themselves doubly out-of-pocket: a successful action against an indemnified director can cost the shareholders more in recovery and reimbursement than they lost through having their corporation badly run.

Directors' duty of care has also been undermined by the US 'business judgement rule'. It ' … gives directors a rebuttable presumption of correctness, meaning that anyone challenging a business decision has the burden of proving that it violates fiduciary standards.'[30]. Historically invoked to prevent legal challenges to anything that can be considered within the conduct of a corporation's ordinary business, it did, until recently, prevent all challenges of, e.g., directors' remuneration.

Some US states further limit directors' accountability, by requiring lengthy, staggered terms for boards of directors. When

---

28 According to Manifest, the proxy voting service, 76 directors of FTSE 100 companies are on two-year rolling contracts. Mark Court and Nic Hopkins, 'Investors increase pressure against two-year contracts', *The Times*, 18 March 2003, p. 30. Cf. the Higgs Report recommendation (B.1.8): 'Notice or contract periods should be set at one year or less.'

29 For a review of the many ways in which they have been undermined, see Monks and Minnow, *PA*, *op. cit.*, especially Chapter 3.

30 *Ibid.*, p. 88.

terms are staggered, only some of the directors can be replaced at any election, regardless of the number of shares acquired. The other directors are effectively freed from any need to be accountable to the shareholders until their terms expire.[31] In such circumstances, even the threat of takeovers can have little effect.

In summary, then, directors' effectiveness in protecting shareholder interests is considerably less in practice than it is in theory. Lacking a proper understanding of their distinctive duties, and the qualities and resources needed to fulfil them, directors can be seriously defective as corporate governors. The ways in which they are selected, appointed and remunerated can make directors too dependent on the managements they are meant to oversee, and provide a positive incentive for directors to undermine shareholders' interests. And when they fail to fulfil their fiduciary duties, there is little that shareholders can do.

Shareholders' shortcomings

But it is not just the defects of corporate elections and directors that hinder corporate accountability. The way that shareholders relate to their companies and to each other, and the way that institutional shareholders relate to their own constituents, also represent significant obstacles to the enforcement of shareholders' theoretical rights. Though activism is commonly recommended as

---

31   See Lucian Arye Bebchuk, John C. Coates and Guhan Subramanian, 'The Powerful Antitakeover Force of Staggered Boards: Further Findings and a Reply to Symposium Participants', *Stanford Law Review*, 55(3), 2002, pp. 885–917, http://papers.ssrn.com/paper.taf?abstract_id=360840 and 'The Powerful Antitakeover Force of Staggered Boards: Theory, Evidence, and Policy', *Stanford Law Review*, 54, 2002, pp. 887–951, http://papers.ssrn.com/paper.taf?abstract_id=304388.

the best way for shareholders to protect their interests[32], in practice it is often easier, cheaper and more rational to sell shares than to attempt active corporate governance.

Contrary to popular belief, the main problem is not that fund managers are ill-equipped to manage corporations. They may well be, but management is not what is required of them. Exercising the rights of ownership requires holding directors to account, not doing the job of a director … still less doing the job of a manager. Just as direction is conceptually distinct from management, ownership is conceptually distinct from them both. Good corporate governance simply requires that shareholders know what they want from the companies that they own, and that they exert the effort necessary to keep directors accountable for achieving those goals.[33] Unfortunately, even that is often not done.

A serious impediment to shareholders' enforcing accountability is the lack of information they have about corporate performance. Shareholders' ability to get information about their companies is doubly limited. Executives determine the flow of information to directors, and directors determine the content and timing of information that is distributed to shareholders.

---

32 See, e.g., the ISC code published in October 2002: *The Responsibilities of Institutional Shareholders and Agents: Statement of Principles*.

33 'Institutional investors, especially those who are investing other people's money, have an obligation to be intelligent shareholders. They must read and vote proxies, understand the factors affecting a company's business, and make their views on important issues known to managers and directors. Second, institutional investors should put pressure on directors to be more responsive to shareholder concerns about long-term strategies and the productive use of corporate assets.' 3 April 1990 letter to shareholders from Edward C. ('Ned') Johnson III, controlling shareholder of Fidelity, the largest privately held money management group in the world at that time, and the founder of the modern mutual fund industry. Quoted in Monks and Minnow, *PA, op. cit.*, p. 205.

Although stock exchange regulations in well-ordered jurisdictions require that material price-sensitive information be made available to the market as soon as it is known, managements and boards have considerable leeway in deciding what is material or likely to influence prices; they can decide what they officially know and when they know it.

Even when information about the corporation is available, the costs of acting on that information can be prohibitive. In the United States, communications amongst shareholders are subject to complex regulation; compliance is both difficult and expensive. Consequently, shareholders are subject to what is known as the 'collective choice problem', a variant of the 'prisoners' dilemma'. Though all the shareholders might benefit from working together to improve the governance of their corporation, in the absence of communication, each shareholder working alone is likely to be better off by selling out. The very dispersion of ownership that makes corporate governance necessary, also makes it difficult.

Even when, as in the UK, shareholders often know at least some of their fellow shareholders, and are not legally barred from communicating with them, there remain significant obstacles to cooperative action.[34] If a diligent shareholder suspects trouble in any of his investments, it normally makes more sense to sell out than to alert the other investors. Informing them would lose him any intelligence advantage he might have. And since his rivals would, in any case, most likely respond by immediately selling their shares, telling them might well depress the price the diligent investor could obtain when he wanted to sell.

Any shareholder who attempts corrective action is likely to

34 For a graphic description of the obstacles facing UK institutional investors, see Alistair Blair, 'A coalition versus a dictator', *Financial Times*, 27 May 1992, p. 13.

bear the full costs of such action on his own. And those costs can go far beyond the considerable out-of-pocket expenses of compiling and analysing corporate information. An investor who is known to be active or critical may find it harder to get honest answers in future; he will thus be at a disadvantage when it comes to making informed investment decisions. The critical investor may also suffer commercial reprisals from the companies in which he takes an active interest; managements are unlikely to award pension fund management or insurance or banking business to institutions that have given them a hard time. Furthermore, an investor who takes the trouble to develop an in-depth understanding of a corporation runs the risk of becoming 'contaminated' by inside information. When that happens, then even if he concludes that there is nothing he can do to improve corporate performance, he will be barred from selling his shares by insider trading regulation. Finally, if an investor accumulates a large enough stake to make a difference to corporate governance, he may be forced by UK regulation governing takeovers to bid for the entire company.

Unfortunately, the substantial obstacles to and costs of active shareholding[35] are not matched by comparable rewards. While the costs of activism are borne by the active shareholder, whatever corporate governance benefits may result are enjoyed by all the shareholders; investors who have remained passive get them as a free bonus[36]. The possibility that simply by waiting one may benefit from someone else's effort makes activism less rational.

Even more fundamentally, most sorts of institutional shareholder get *no* direct benefit from attempting to improve corporate

---

35   For a summary of the obstacles, see Bernard. S. Black, 'Shareholder activism re-examined', *Michigan Law Review*, Vol. 89, December 1990, pp. 520–608.

36   The classic 'free-rider' problem.

governance. And that is because they are not the ultimate owners of the shares whose value would increase: they are merely intermediaries. Moreover, they are intermediaries who are seldom if ever held accountable for improving corporate governance. While institutional investors are typically penalised for taking risks, they are seldom rewarded for getting superior investment returns.

Consider the main types of institutional investor. Investment trusts are corporations, whose shareholders are typically individual investors. Those individuals are no more able or likely than any other to hold their agents to account. Moreover, the directors of investment trusts have often been closely connected to the fund manager[37], and thus subject to substantial conflicts of interest.[38] It is perhaps noteworthy that investment trusts often trade at a discount to net asset value.[39]

Unlike investment trusts, unit trusts are real trusts, as are bank-administered trust funds and most pension funds; their trustees are, therefore, obliged to manage them in the best interests of the beneficiaries. Trustees are, however, typically evaluated on procedural criteria that have nothing to do with the performance or the governance of their investments. So long as they appoint

---

37 Jean Eaglesham, 'Fund managers in the firing line', *Financial Times*, 24 July 1997, p. 28.

38 The conflict is most prominent when investment trusts trade at a discount to their net asset value: the interests of shareholders wanting to wind up the trust to realise the value of the underlying assets are at odds with the interests of managers wanting the trust to survive, so that they will continue to get a management fee. See Jean Eaglesham, 'Investment trust holders lose confidence in sector', *Financial Times*, 18 April 1998, p. 20.

39 As of 31 August 2003, the size-weighted average discount for AITC conventional trusts was 11.9 per cent. Source: Association of Investment Trust companies, Monthly Information Reports,
http://www.aitc.co.uk/files/KF%2031%20August%202003.pdf.

professional fund managers and do not embezzle, they are normally deemed to have fulfilled their obligations.[40]

The beneficiaries on behalf of whom trust assets are owned, and whose interests trustees are supposed to serve, have little if any power to hold the trustees accountable.[41] They seldom know whether their trustees have voted the shares that they nominally own, far less how they have voted them. When investment of the pension fund has been delegated to a fund manager, voting information is even less accessible.

Despite requiring a percentage of member-nominated trustees, the 1995 Pensions Act (UK) did little either to increase the independence of company pension schemes from management dominance or to increase accountability. From July 2000, an amendment has required that if a pension fund has a policy on exercising the rights (including voting rights) attaching to investments, that policy be disclosed as part of the Statement of Investment Principles.[42] The minimum three year period for

40 'The trustee has no economic interest whatsoever in the quality of the voting decision, beyond avoiding liability. No enforcement action has ever been brought and no damages ever awarded for breach of duty in voting proxies. Trustees earn no incentive compensation, no matter how much energy and skill they devote to ownership responsibilities. And, crucially, the corporation knows how the trustee votes, whereas [the owner] has no idea. The trustee has nothing to lose from routing votes [voting] with management and everything to gain.' Monks and Minnow, *PA, op. cit.*, pp. 36–7; see also pp. 44, 189, 251. Although the UK Myners Report (*Institutional Investment in the United Kingdom: A Review*, March 2001) identified a number of deficiencies in the conduct of trustees, it did not address the issue of how trustees could better be required to fulfil their fiduciary responsibilities.

41 Until recently, members of company pension schemes had little choice even as to whether to participate in their employers' schemes.

42 The Occupational Pension Schemes (Investment, and Assignment, Forfeiture, Bankruptcy, etc.) Amendment Regulations 1999 also requires that Statements of Investment Principles explain the extent (if at all) to which social, environmental

appointments makes it difficult to review or replace pension trustees. The requirement for member-nominated trustees to be members of the scheme shows a dangerous acceptance of the 'constituency' theory of representation. And the need for them to be approved and removed only with the consent of all the other trustees limits their independence.

In the US, there are even graver obstacles to active corporate governance. Mutual funds, the US equivalents of unit trusts, are inhibited by the regulations governing their tax advantages[43] from being active investors. And pension funds administered for the benefit of US federal employees are prohibited by statute[44] from directly exercising voting rights in respect of shares held by the fund. So two of the largest classes of institutional investor are effectively barred from exercising the most basic kind of corporate governance.

Insurance companies also have little to gain from shareholder activism and much to lose, because of the varied commercial relationships they often have with the companies in which they invest. Insurance companies that are active as shareholders may well find themselves at a disadvantage both as suppliers of risk insurance to the companies they challenge, and as suppliers of investment products to those companies' pension funds. And where insurance companies are large takers of debt private placements (as they are in the US, for example), their own

---

or ethical considerations are taken into account in the selection, retention and realisation of investments.

43 Internal Revenue Code Subchapter M; see Monks and Minnow, *PA, op. cit.*, p. 201.

44 The Federal Employees' Retirement System Act of 1986 (FERSA) provides that voting rights are delegated to the administrator appointed by the trustees.

investment opportunities may be jeopardised. It is therefore not surprising that, like most institutional investors, insurance companies generally observe what is known as the 'Wall Street Rule': they either sell, or vote with management ... regardless of the effect on share value.

But aren't fund managers evaluated by investors on the basis of their investment performance? Indeed they are. The fund managers employed by pension funds, unit and investment trusts are normally assessed on the basis of their historical portfolio returns compared with other fund managers. But this does not mean that they are held accountable for the corporate governance of the companies in their portfolios. The beneficial owners of the funds managed will typically have no information about the extent to which, or the ways in which, the fund managers has voted in corporate elections.[45]

Moreover, portfolio returns are typically influenced far more substantially and directly by stock selection and asset allocation than they are by corporate governance. Insofar as the performance of particular shares is disappointing, it will therefore normally be more sensible for fund managers to alter the composition of their portfolios than to engage in shareholder activism, especially when activism risks costing them liquidity as well as access to information and ancillary business.

Finally, many of the techniques used to protect operational managements of other businesses from accountability, have also been employed by fund managers in their relations with institutional investors. Long-term rolling contracts, for example, can make it prohibitively expensive for an institutional investor to

---

45   See Chapter 4, note 13 above (p. 84).

replace a fund manager[46], even if the performance of the fund is grossly inadequate. Fund managers are therefore seldom held properly accountable for the performance of the portfolios entrusted to them.

In summary, then, there are substantial obstacles which prevent shareholders from keeping their corporations and corporate agents accountable. So long as the gains from improving corporate governance are slower and smaller than those obtainable from portfolio adjustment, shareholder activism will not be the rational choice.

---

46 This is a point that critics of the 'short-termism' supposedly engendered by short-term contracts conveniently forget.

Section 3
Conventional Correctives Challenged

So the traditional Anglo-American system of corporate governance is far from perfect: in practice, many of the mechanisms that are supposed to ensure accountability fail to do so. As a result, the costs of attempting to maintain accountability can be high. Contrary to popular belief, however, the standard alternatives are, unfortunately, even worse: far from improving accountability to owners, they make it irrelevant or impossible.

This section will examine three alternatives to the current Anglo-American system. Chapter 5 will evaluate the much praised corporate governance systems of Germany and Japan. Chapter 6 will analyse the meaning, operations and implications of the popular stakeholder approach. Chapter 7 will consider the consequences of more stringent corporate regulation. The section will show that far from overcoming the difficulties that afflict the Anglo-American model, the German and Japanese alternatives, stakeholding, and regulation all suffer from problems that are even more severe. Considered as means of securing genuine corporate governance, the supposed improvements are both theoretically and practically inferior to the traditional Anglo-American system.

5 THE DEFECTS OF THE GERMAN AND JAPANESE SYSTEMS

One of the strangest features of British commentary on business and society over the last two decades has been the seemingly uncritical preference for most things German and Japanese. Even when those economies were outperforming the British, it was open to question whether the post-war successes of Germany and Japan were achieved because of, or in spite of, their distinctive systems[1]. When those systems are underperforming, however, and when they are increasingly under attack even in their domestic markets[2], preferring the traditional German or Japanese systems is positively perverse[3].

Though there are undoubtedly lessons to be learned from the Germans and the Japanese, those who advocate their systems as

---

1   Samuel Brittan, 'Economic Viewpoint: Silly slogans of stakeholders', *Financial Times*, 7 September 1995, p. 22.
2   Consider the verdict of the head of the first German Commission on corporate governance, Prof. Dr Theodor Baums: 'The regulatory mechanisms of German corporate governance ... compared to other legal systems, they are rigid and inflexible and do not provide sufficient protection for investors. These shortcomings must be rectified.' 'The End of Germany, Inc.? Corporate legal reform in Germany', in Deutsche *Börse, German Capital Markets Achievements and Challenges*, White Paper, 2003 (henceforth '*Börse* White Paper'), p. 39. See also Yanai Hiroyuki, 'Re-examining Corporate Governance in Japan', *Journal of Japanese Trade & Industry* (henceforth '*JJTI*'), 1 March 2003, and Barney Jopson, 'Japanese warming to activist cause', *Financial Times*, 2 June 2003.
3   Consider, e.g, OECD criticisms of German governance; reported in Peter Norman, 'Corporate change urged on Germany', *Financial Times*, 30 August 1995, p. 2.

ways of improving corporate governance seem guilty of the offence for which Socrates was executed: they would make the worse appear the better cause.

Claims to German or Japanese superiority at corporate governance are *prima facie* dubious, considering the continuing stream of German and Japanese corporate losses and disasters. Problems at major German companies that have been serious enough to attract international media attention have included embezzlement, uncontrolled trading, fraud, insider trading, massive hidden losses and industrial espionage. The story of Japanese governance is no more reassuring. Consider the parlous state of the banking system, and the frequent reports of illegal payments to gangsters, illegal *tobashi*[4] deals, alleged bribery of government officials, uncontrolled securities and commodities trading and cover-ups, and sexual harassment[5]. According to the Corporate Auditors' Association of Japan, nearly one third of major Japanese companies were either guilty of improper business practices or involved in scandal during the ten years to 1997.[6] The (illegal) Japanese institution of *sokaiya* – professional extortionists who threaten to reveal sensitive company information – could not even exist, far less flourish, without a culture of secrecy.

German and Japanese companies have not only displayed a conspicuous lack of control, but have been markedly disappoint-

4   Transactions designed to conceal losses, typically by transferring them to other accounts; Bethan Hutton, '"Dirty laundry" may get a public airing', *Financial Times*, 26 November 1997, p. 8.

5   In recent years, more than 100 Japanese corporations in the US have been sued on grounds of sexual harassment and racial prejudice. Robert Taylor, 'Japanese to receive advice on equality', *Financial Times*, 14 April 1997, p. 12.

6   Gwen Robinson, 'Japanese companies admit bad behaviour', *Financial Times*, 11 April 1997, p. 6.

ing in delivering shareholder value. Media attention may have focused on US scandals, but while it did, the German and Japanese equity markets plummeted. Compared with their peaks in March 2000, the German DAX index fell 66.6 per cent to February 2003 and the Japanese Nikkei fell 56.9 per cent, versus drops of 43.7 per cent for the US Wilshire 500 and 45.9 per cent for the FTSE 100.[7]

The low returns on equity characteristic of the German and Japanese markets are, however, hardly surprising considering the very low priority given to shareholder value and individual enterprise in them both. In Japan, generating returns for shareholders is less important than increasing market share[8] or maintaining employment[9]; the primary function of shareholdings is to assure markets and supplies[10], not to obtain capital. In Germany, despite major legislative changes to bring corporate governance closer to the Anglo-American model[11], the main function of shareholding is

---

7   OECD, *Highlights of Recent Trends in Financial Markets*, April 2003, Table 1, p. 11. The UK comparision was against a peak in December 1999.

8   According to one survey, only 5 per cent of Japanese managers consider their company's share price to be important; 'A Survey of Japanese Finance', *The Economist*, 28 June 1997, p. 14.

9   'Japan on the brink', *The Economist*, 11 April 1998, p. 19.

10 Nicholas Kochan and Michael Syrett, *New Directions in Corporate Governance*, Business International Limited, 1991, p. 91.

11 Notably the Act on the Control and Transparency in Enterprises (*Gesetz zur Kontrolle und Transparenz im Unternehmensbereich*; '*KonTraG*'; effective 1 May 1998), the Act on Further Reform of the Stock Corporation and Accounting Law, Transparency and Disclosures (*Gesetz zur weiteren Reform des Aktien- und Bilanzrechts, zu Transparenz und Publizität*; '*TransPuG*'; passed on 26 February 2002), the Securities Acquisition and Takeover Act ('*WpÜG*'; effective 1 January 2002), and 1 July 2002 amendments to the Securities Trading Act ('WpHg': http://www.bafin.de/gesetze/wphg_e.htm). The German Corporate Governance ('Cromme') Code is imposed through a 'comply or explain' requirement incorporated into section 161 of the Stock Corporation Act ('*AktG*') by the *TransPuG*. In addition, on 1 May 2002 the federal watchdogs for banking, insurance, and securities trading were amalgamated to form the Federal Financial Supervisory Authority ('*BaFin*').

still to cement relationships and consolidate power. The German language does not even have an expression for 'shareholder value': the English phrase is used, emphasising the concept's foreign origin and alien nature.[12] Even that usage was largely abandoned in response to labour union pressure; the few prominent German proponents of shareholder value were forced to speak instead of *unternehmenswertsteigerung*, 'raising the enterprise's value'.[13]

It is indicative that, despite some much publicised advocacy of shareholder value by a few German companies and commentators, and the need to attract investors to what was Europe's largest ever initial public offering, the Deutsche Telekom prospectus still put 'generating attractive returns for shareholders' *fifth* in the company's list of objectives. That was so even though the offering was explicitly described by a director of Deutsche Bank as Germany's 'last big chance to establish an equity culture'.[14] Shareholder returns nevertheless came after strengthening domestic market position, achieving foreign growth, increasing sales, cash flow and earnings, and strengthening the balance sheet .... [15]

When shareholders rank so low in corporate priorities, it is hardly surprising that 'Germans spend more money on bananas than they do on equities'.[16] The number of German quoted com-

---

12 Stefan Wagstyl, 'Crumbs from the table', *Financial Times*, 25 September 1996, p. 27.

13 Jürgen Schrempp of Daimler-Benz and Ulrich Hartmann of Veba; Lex, 'Shareholder Value', *Financial Times*, 22 November 1996, p. 20.

14 Rolf Breuer, quoted in 'Launching Deutsche Telekom', *The Economist*, 26 October 1996, p. 105.

15 Tony Jackson, 'Record issue stirs investor enthusiasm', *Financial Times*, 23 October 1996, p. 26.

16 Norbert Walter, chief economist at Deutsche Bank, addressing a pensions conference; quoted in Norma Cohen, 'Restrictionist governments may fail to see the folly of their ways' *Financial Times*, 24 June 1996, p. 22.

panies is small[17], relatively few shares are freely traded[18], and share ownership is both far below the American and British levels[19] and is decreasing[20]. Germans prefer to invest their monies in bonds, bank deposits or insurance.[21]

Unfortunately, space does not allow a full review of the workings of the German and Japanese models of corporate governance[22] here. Although the German and Japanese models are often lumped together in contrast to the Anglo-American model, they are, in fact, as different from each other as they are from it. Despite substantial recent reforms, German corporations are structurally

---

17 678 vs. 1,745 in the UK; *Survey: German Banking and Finance, Financial Times*, 29 May 1996, p. 2. As of 2002, it was still 'about 700'. Ninety-nine per cent of German companies with sales of between DM25 million and DM250 million are privately owed; 'Mittelstand', Lex, *Financial Times*, 4 November 1996, p. 24.

18 Market capitalisation as a percentage of GDP (2001) was 58.1 per cent in Germany versus 152.0 per cent in the UK, 136.3 per cent in the US and 55.4 per cent in Japan; *Börse* White Paper, *op. cit.*, p. 79.

19 By 1996 only 5 per cent of Germans owned equities ('Mittelstand', *op. cit.*). Mass equity ownership in Germany started only with the partial privatisation of Deutsche Telekom in 1996. By 2001, Germans had an average €4,780 per capita in mutual funds, significantly less than Americans with €25,000 and Britons with €7,000. According to the Deutsche Aktieninstitut, the number of direct and indirect shareholders in Germany rose to 13.4 million in the first half of 2001 from 11.3 million in the corresponding period of 2000. Tony Barber, 'Reforms set to further reshape capitalism', *Survey – German Banking & Finance, Financial Times*, 15 October 2001, p. 6.

20 *Börse* White Paper, *op. cit.*, p. 30.

21 In 2002, sales of fixed interest securities in Germany totalled €818,735 million, compared with €11,434 million for shares. Federal Statistics Office Germany, www.destatis.de/basis/e/banktab5.htm, updated 5 May 2003.

22 For an overview of the workings of the German and Japanese models, see, for example, Robert A. G. Monks and Nell Minnow, *Corporate Governance*, 2nd edn, Blackwell, 2001 (henceforth '*CG*'); Robert I. Tricker, *International Corporate Governance: Text, Readings and Cases*, Prentice Hall, 1994; Jonathan Charkham, *Keeping Good Company: A Study of Corporate Governance in Five Countries*, Oxford University Press, 1995; and Kochan and Syrett, *New Directions, op. cit.*.

unlike Anglo-American ones. Japanese companies, in contrast, are structurally similar to Anglo-American companies, but employ those structures in characteristically different ways, and in pursuit of different ends.

The most distinctive feature of the German model of corporate governance is the two-tier board structure, which dates back to the 1870s and is required by German law[23]: German companies[24] must have both a management board and a supervisory board. The management board consists of executives of the company and is responsible for managing it; the supervisory board, which may not include executives, is responsible for appointing and supervising the management board. Though the supervisory board is elected at the general meeting of shareholders, between 33 per cent and 50 per cent of directors must by law be employee representatives. Supervisory boards also typically contain representatives of firms with close functional relations with the company, including suppliers, customers and bankers.

Japanese corporations, in contrast, have a unitary board structure similar to that of Anglo-American companies. Unlike the Anglo-American board, however, the typical Japanese board is hierarchical and very large[25]; it consists almost exclusively of managers of the company itself and of firms related to it. A distinctive feature of Japanese corporations is that they tend to be members

---

23 The basic law on stock corporations, the Stock Corporation Act, *Aktiengesetz* of 6 September 1965 (*Bundesgesetzblatt*); Prof. Dr Theodor Baums, 'Corporate Governance in Germany – System and Current Developments', 2000 (henceforth 'CGG'), http://www.germanbusinesslaw.de/inhalt.htm.

24 All AGs and GmbHs with more than 5,000 employees; Monks and Minnow, *CG*, *op. cit.*, p. 287.

25 Toyota's board, for example, consisted of 58 directors, all of whom were executives of the company. Mariko Sanchanta, 'Toyota to halve board members', *Financial Times*, 31 March 2003, p. 28. See also note 60 below.

of a 'family' of firms connected by a shared history, complementary operations, and interlocking shareholdings.

What is significant for the purposes of this discussion, is that when these alternative models of corporate governance are evaluated against the same criteria that are commonly used to criticise the Anglo-American model, they both fare worse than it does. The few genuine advantages that the German and Japanese systems do afford are compatible with, and could be better secured within, the Anglo-American model. The disadvantages of the German and Japanese systems, however, go far beyond including most of the same democratic deficits, directors' defects, and shareholders' shortcomings as the Anglo-American system. Unlike the Anglo-American model, they are integral parts of systems that reflect a profound distrust of, and lack of respect for, individual liberties. The German and Japanese systems are often praised precisely because they are associated with social ends that many commentators prefer.

Ostensible superiority

Consider the ways in which the German or Japanese systems are commonly believed to be superior. Whereas, it is asserted, ailing Anglo-American corporations are forced into bankruptcy by their bankers, German companies are routinely rescued by them; whereas Anglo-American companies constantly have to defend themselves from 'immoral' takeover bids, German and Japanese companies can concentrate on perfecting their products; whereas Anglo-American workers live in fear of redundancy, German and Japanese workers enjoy secure jobs for life. The standard argument is that the non-Anglo-American systems should be preferred because they are 'long-termist' and 'inclusive' in their outlook; unlike the Anglo-American system, which is damagingly 'short-termist' and 'adversarial', the other systems are, it is alleged, better at achieving consensus and social stability.

The first thing to be noted about this argument, is that its premises are highly questionable. As has already been argued, the 'evils' that it associates with the Anglo-American system – notably 'short-termism' and takeovers – are not necessarily, or even typically, immoral. The supposed benefits are equally questionable. 'Long-termism' has been associated with pervasive misallocation of resources and sustained failures. The security that the argument attributes to Germany and Japan is not available to significant subsections of their populations. German guest workers do not enjoy job security; nor do most Japanese nationals, men[26] or women[27]. Furthermore, even when they are available, the supposed benefits are at best a mixed blessing. They are achieved at the cost of a paternalism and comprehensive protectionism that not only undermines accountability and shareholder value, but also inhibits innovation and infringes individual liberty. It is no coincidence that activities as fundamental and as personal as shopping and contraception have been highly restricted in Germany[28] and Japan[29].

---

26 Traditionally, lifetime employment has applied only to *circa* 20 per cent of the men employed by large companies; Sheryl WuDunn, 'Japan: Facade of Job Security Slowly Cracks', *International Herald Tribune*, 13 June 1996, p. 18.

27 *Ibid.* In Japan, 'The vast majority of women are still employed on "*ippanshoku*" (freely translated as "zero-career contracts") and it is common to put to these employees that they should resign upon marriage or childbirth at the latest.' Letter to the editor from Ludwig Kanzler, 'Japan's female workforce', *Financial Times*, 31 August 1996, p. 6.

28 Before 1996, the *Ladenschlügesetz* (store-closing law) prevented Germans from shopping after 6.30 p.m. weekdays or 2 p.m. on most Saturdays. Saturday

Moreover, even if – counterfactually – its premises and its conclusions were true, the standard argument offered by proponents of the German and Japanese systems is only remotely about corporate governance. Although presented in the guise of corporate governance, the argument is not that the German and Japanese systems provide better methods of keeping corporations to their official objectives. Rather, the argument's champions are simply endorsing a set of broad social, economic and political values[30] – consensus, community, 'inclusiveness', harmony – that they associate with (post-war) Germany and Japan.

For this approach to constitute a valid argument in support of the German or Japanese systems of corporate governance, its proponents would have to show three things. First, they would have to establish that the values they prefer are indeed the most important social, economic and political values, necessarily to be preferred to those others – including justice and individual liberty, for example – with which they are often incompatible. This requires more than showing that the 'inclusive' values are sometimes, or even commonly, favoured. It also requires more than showing that those values may be useful in promoting certain sorts of corporate objectives. It requires demonstrating that the 'inclusive' values *should* be preferred, that they are *morally* superior.

Second, proponents of the other systems would have to show

---

shopping until 8 p.m. has only been permitted since 1 June 2003; Sunday shopping is still illegal. And pending parliamentary approval of proposed reforms, close-out sales remain restricted to two specified fortnights each year. Associated Press Worldstream, 'German government approves plan to loosen restrictions on store sales', 7 May 2003.

29 Japan was the last nation in the United Nations to allow use of the contraceptive pill, approving it only in September 1999, almost forty years after it was approved in the US. 'Japanese Pill', Leader, *Financial Times*, 7 June 1999, p. 15.

30 The 'inclusive' values.

that the 'inclusive' values are genuinely better served in Germany and Japan, a fact that looks ever less plausible following the Asian economic crisis and German economic decline. Third, they would have to show that the 'inclusive' values are a necessary consequence, or at least a necessary concomitant, of the German and Japanese models of corporate governance.

Until and unless that ambitious project is undertaken, however, the superiority of the other corporate governance systems must depend on their ability to fulfil straightforward corporate governance functions. A systematic evaluation of the alternative models would involve measuring each model against all of the criteria employed in Chapter 4 above, in the criticism of the Anglo-American model. Unfortunately, there is no space for that comprehensive project here. This discussion will, instead, focus on assessing the degree to which the most prominent features of the German and Japanese systems enhance or undermine accountability to the official corporate objectives.[31]

The German system does seem, at least initially, to have two features that offer improved accountability to owners. First, thanks to the two-tier board structure, the German system apparently provides a clear separation between the responsibilities of directors and managers: the different functions of the two groups are reflected in the separate boards on which they sit. But while such clarity of responsibility is indeed a good thing,

---

31 Because so much in the German model is required by law, and because Japanese custom is relatively uniform, the discussion will consider actual German and Japanese practice. Because Anglo-Saxon jurisdictions, in contrast, characteristically allow significant variations, comparisons will be with what the Anglo-Saxon model theoretically allows, not with particular local implementations of it. It is, in any case, the theoretical model of Anglo-Saxon corporate governance that is often under attack by those who prefer the German and Japanese models.

it is a good feature that is wholly compatible with the Anglo-American model. It could as well be achieved by having the unitary board consist exclusively of non-executives. There is no requirement, in principle or in law, to have executives on the board; their talents and expertise could be fully captured for the company by including them on executive committees of various sorts. To the extent, therefore, that a sharp separation of responsibilities were truly wanted, it could be obtained perfectly well within the Anglo-American system.

A second German mechanism that ought to strengthen accountability to owners, is the fact that members of the German management board owe their positions to the supervisory board, and not *vice versa*. In principle, this should help to ensure the independence of the supervisory board, because the appointments of supervisory directors do not depend on the management. And it should also help improve the quality of the management board, which must satisfy the standards set by independent supervisors. Admirable though those objectives are, however, they could equally well be achieved within the Anglo-American system. They would result if appointments of senior executives required board approval, and if directors were nominated as well as elected by shareholders.[32]

In practice, of course, things are different. But they are different in both systems. Even enshrining German corporate governance requirements in law does not prevent nominations for the board of supervisors actually coming from German management boards … it does not even prevent members of the management board

---

32 Although the latter is illegal in some jurisdictions, these mechanisms are none-theless perfectly compatible with the Anglo-American model.

from nominating themselves.[33] When that is so, then supervisory independence and management competence can be compromised as much as when executives influence the choice of Anglo-American board members. Once again, therefore, there is no reason to prefer the German model.

Actual inferiority

There are, moreover, many reasons why it is inferior to the Anglo-American system. Consider conflicts of interest, for example. Although German supervisory boards have no executive members, they are nonetheless plagued by conflicts of interest far greater than those found in Anglo-American companies. Supervisory directors are typically chosen either to reinforce relationships with firms that work closely with the corporation, or to comply with the legal requirement for worker representation; directors from both groups are expected to promote their constituency's particular interests. Accordingly, supervisory directors normally have personal, professional or commercial interests that directly conflict with those of the company's shareholders.[34]

Suffering from such structural conflicts of interest, supervisory directors can be seriously constrained from providing necessary criticism or even useful supervision of the management board. Their external interests – as sources of finance or sources of la-

33   Consider Hilmar Kopper, chairman of the management board of Deutsche Bank. Having retired early in recognition of the disasters suffered by the bank during his management of it, he put himself forward to become head of Deutsche's supervisory board …. John Gapper and Andrew Fisher, 'Deutsche's model of the universal banker', *Financial Times*, 31 October 1996, p. 17.

34   Directors from banks, for example, are likely to have a vested interest in promoting debt-supported size rather than profitability in the companies they control.

bour, as suppliers or customers or professional advisors – might be jeopardised if they challenged the conduct of management. Candid comment can be further inhibited by the presence on the board of employee representatives[35], and by the fact that board memberships and shareholdings[36] are often reciprocal: directors refrain from judging, lest they in turn be judged. Although such conflicts of interest occasionally afflict Anglo-American companies, they are endemic in Germany and Japan.

They do, however, tend to be evaluated differently. Whereas Anglo-American boards are criticised if their non-executives have ever been executives – even in the distant past, and for wholly unrelated firms – German supervisory boards are routinely applauded for including the current directors of closely related or even competing firms. The same features that commentators criticise in the Anglo-American system as conflicts of interest, capable of undermining directors' independence and ability to monitor effectively, are praised as signs of 'inclusiveness' and sources of consensus and

---

35 In addition to having dubious competence to tackle strategic issues, employee-elected board members have a propensity to leak measures that they oppose to the media. Bertrand Benoit, 'Is Germany's model finding its level?', *Financial Times*, 5 September 2002, p. 11.

36 Cross-shareholdings tend to insulate firms from the corrective influence of the marketplace even when the firms involved do not formally act as a cartel. Scarce supplies or contracts, for example, are likely to be given to related firms, regardless of whether they would be the most deserving in an open competition. Companies and their shareholders are therefore denied important market feedback. Until recently, companies owned 42 per cent of German equities; Andrew Fisher, 'Euro likely to start equities ball rolling', *Financial Times*, 18 November 1997, p. 3. Since 1 January 2002, sales of corporate holdings have no longer been subject to the capital gains tax that long discouraged divestiture; sales of industrial stakes have, however, been hindered by depressed financial markets. Uta Harnischfeger, 'Grudging moves on corporate transparency', *Financial Times, Survey – Germany: Banking, Finance & Investment*, 12 June 2002, p. 3.

stability when they occur in Germany and Japan. This is evidence not of the superiority of foreign models of corporate governance, but of the operation of a damaging double standard.

Intrinsic conflicts of interest are not the only obstacles to German and Japanese boards' protecting shareholders' interests. The typical ways in which such boards are composed make them unsuited to exercising effective supervision. Japanese boards are normally very large and strictly hierarchical; they consist of managers who have been selected by other, more senior, managers and who are unlikely to criticise their colleagues. Appointments to German supervisory boards are, by law, subject to veto by the other directors[37]: committed proponents of shareholder value are unlikely to be approved by the directors who represent competing interests.

The legally-stipulated size of German supervisory boards also makes it difficult for them to function effectively as supervisory bodies. Required to have between twelve and twenty members, supervisory boards have indeed been so unwieldy that legislation has been proposed to reduce their size, in the hope of increasing their professionalism. Another impediment to proper supervision comes from the large number of directorships[38] which members of German boards, particularly bankers, typically hold: the attention available for each company is necessarily diluted. Even if just two directorships are held, however, the result is likely to be not just a conflict of interest, but a positive conflict of obligation, insofar as the fiduciary duties to different groups collide.

---

37 Kochan and Syrett, *New Directions, op. cit.*, p. 66. It may, however, be possible to override an employee veto in the second round of elections, which requires only a simple majority.

38 Reduced to 10 per person by the *KonTraG*.

Moreover, however popular bankers are as supervisory board members[39], their presence is no guarantee of competent supervision.[40] Like other supervisory directors, bankers tend to be chosen because they represent particular interests, not because they have any particular skill in directing companies. Given their traditional risk aversion and conflicts of interest, bankers are indeed likely to be less well suited even than fund managers for handling complex commercial risks. This may help explain why so many German companies have been disaster-prone despite ostensible supervision by major German banks.

German supervisory boards are also deprived of a standard monitoring tool available to Anglo-American boards: information[41], and especially reliable financial statements designed to show changes in shareholder value. Barred by law from having any involvement in the daily operations of the company, supervisory board members and, *a fortiori* shareholders, are wholly dependent on information provided by the management board. It is therefore essential that financial statements provide relevant and reliable information on company performance. But German financial statements are not designed to do so. Structured more

---

39 According to a report from the German Monopolies Commission (quoted in Kochan and Syrett, *New Directions, op. cit.* p. 71), 75 out of 84 firms had a banker on the supervisory board. In 31 cases, the banker was the chairman of the board; in 18 of those 31 cases the bank was Deutsche Bank.

40 The supervisory boards of the disaster-prone KHD and Metallgesellschaft were headed by Deutsche Bankers; the collapsed Schneider property empire, Daimler-Benz, and Volkswagen also are or have been under the supposed supervision of the country's premier bank/shareholder; see Andrew Fisher, 'Banks under pressure', *Financial Times*, 23 October 1995, *Survey of Germany*, p. iv.

41 Even after the *TransPuG* reforms, for example, the supervisory board is not authorised to consult or examine documents from subsidiaries. Baums, 'The End of Germany Inc.?', *Börse* White Paper, *op. cit.*, p. 45.

to satisfy creditors and tax authorities than to enlighten share-holders, German financial accounts typically paint a picture that is substantially different than that which results from the application of US or UK accounting standards; they obscure, rather than disclose, how well shareholders' objectives have been served. Moreover, before the 1998 enactment of the *Kon-TraG*, auditors of German companies were by law appointed by, and reported to, the management board, not the supervisory board.[42] Until and unless more transparent financial statements become the rule in Germany, German corporate governance is at a distinct disadvantage.

Another fundamental defect of the German and Japanese models of corporate governance, is the extent to which they disregard the legitimate demands of shareholder democracy. In Japan, the AGMs of most companies take place on the same day[43], severely limiting the value of the annual general meeting as a forum for observing and questioning company officials. Ostensibly to minimise the risk of having the meetings disrupted by *sokaiya* (professional extortionists who threaten to reveal sensitive company information), the practice also serves to protect company officials from potentially embarrassing questions – the sorts that Anglo-American companies routinely receive

---

42 Independent audit committees, whose chairmen are not former members of the company's management board, were only recommended in the 2002 Corporate Governance Code; *ibid.*, p. 51.

43 Eighty per cent of Japanese companies hold their shareholder meetings on the same day; over 60 per cent of the AGMs last less than 30 minutes. David Ibison, 'Japanese delight as scandals rock the "American model" ', *Financial Times*, 15 August 2002, p. 12. This is actually an improvement: in 1977, the AGMs of 2,355 companies (including those of 95 per cent of companies listed on the Tokyo Stock Exchange) were held on the same day (27 June); Gillian Tett and Gwen Robinson, 'Dai-Ichi Kangyo Bank executives indicted', *Financial Times*, 27 June 1997, p. 3.

from shareholders and investment analysts, and that they are expected to answer. Holding AGMs on the same day also significantly reduces the value of shareholders' votes, because votes can only be exercised when shareholders are physically present at AGMs. Dissent is further limited by the practice of packing general meetings with complaisant staff shareholders.[44]

In both Germany and Japan, owning even large blocks of stock does not necessarily confer any control. Japanese companies are notorious for denying board membership to foreigners[45], and it remains difficult for overseas investors to exercise their shareholder rights.[46] In Germany, minority shareholders have few rights, and plural voting rights are only now being phased out. The new takeover code still permits supervisory boards to resist takeover bids without reference to the shareholders. Until the *KonTraG*, shareholders of German companies were routinely prevented from exercising more than 5–10 per cent of the company's voting rights, regardless of the percentage of equity that they owned. Such limitations hurt all shareholders: they not only directly disenfranchise major shareholders, but help insulate German companies from the beneficial effects of takeovers. They also reinforce bank domination of German companies.

Banks influence German companies in three main ways. They directly own between 5 and 7.5 per cent of the shares

---

44 William Dawkins, 'Corporate Japan passes the AGM test', *Financial Times*, 28 June 1996, p. 33.

45 T. Boone Pickens, for example, was unable to acquire a seat on the board of Koito Manufacturing even though he owned 26 per cent of the company and campaigned actively to become a director. Tricker, *International Corporate Governance, op. cit.*, p. 22.

46 Florian Gimbel, 'ICGN calls for voting overhaul', *Financial Times*, 5 May 2003, *FT Report – FT Fund Management*, p. 2.

outstanding.[47] They have representatives on the supervisory boards of most companies.[47] And in their capacity as voting agent for other shareholders, banks have exercised control over *circa* 50–55 per cent of the shares of German companies.[47] Although voting agents are required to solicit the views of the beneficial owners, in the absence of instructions they are relatively[48] free to vote the shares in their own interests. At least prior to the *KonTraG*, in 22 of the 32 largest German companies, the banks regularly controlled enough votes to appoint all the shareholder representatives to the supervisory board.[49] But as already indicated, banks' interests are often at odds with those of the shareholders; banks are not necessarily either disposed or equipped to protect shareholders' interests.

Even more significantly, banks' freedom to vote the shares they administer applies even in respect of their own AGMs. Consequently, the banks which control so much of German industry seem themselves effectively not to be accountable to anyone.[50] Far from improving accountability to shareholders, the German system thus effectively eliminates it for a major section of the economy.

---

47 In 31 of the 32 largest German companies, banks control more than 50 per cent of the votes. Prof. Dr Theodor Baums, 'Corporate Governance in Germany: The Role of the Banks', *American Journal of Comparative Law*, 1992, p. 503; reported in Jean Du Plessis, 'Corporate Governance and the Dominant Role Played by the Banks in Germany', *The Corporate Governance Quarterly* (HK), 2(1), March 1996, p. 25. See also Kochan and Syrett, *New Directions, op. cit.*, pp. 68–70.

48 Although banks that own more than 5 per cent of a company's equity and vote those shares are banned by the *KonTraG* from exercising open-ended proxies granted by clients, banks that desist from voting their own shares, or have specific instructions from the clients, may vote the proxies.

49 Baums, 'The Role of the Banks', *op. cit.*, p. 507.

50 Ekkehart Boehmer, 'Who controls Germany? An exploratory analysis', *Arbeitspapier* Nr. 71, 15 October 1998; downloadable from http://www.germanbusinesslaw.de/inhalt.htm.

But even this is not the most fundamental defect of the German model. The problem is not just that, in practice, it is difficult or costly for shareholders of German companies to keep their corporations accountable. The worst flaw of the German model is that it actively prevents shareholders from determining corporate ends.

The restriction starts with the German constitution. Expressing the 'social market' philosophy that has characterised German public life since World War II, the German constitution[51] requires that property be used to serve 'the public weal'.[52] The fundamental free-market presumption, that property may freely be used to serve its owner's interests, is therefore denied at the start.[53] The authoritarian German approach continues in corporate regulation, which officially stipulates the form of most corporate structures. Whereas in Anglo-American jurisdictions the law typically stipulates only a minimal framework[54], in Germany most corporate features are laid down by law. So much, indeed, is mandated that there is little room for even unanimous votes of shareholders to affect German corporate structures.

Moreover, the particular corporate forms specified by German law restrict the ability of shareholders to determine corporate

---

51 Article 14(2). Charkham, *Keeping Good Company, op. cit.*, p. 10.
52 According to Prof. Dr Theodor Baums, Chairman of the German Federal Government's first Commission on Corporate Governance and Company Law Reform, 'management may and must take the interests of the employees, creditors, and the community at large into account.' CGG, *op. cit.*.
53 The fact that owners' interests both constitute a substantial part of, and serve, the common weal, and that limitations are imposed by, e.g., health and safety regulation in Anglo-American jurisdictions, does not make the German interference any less onerous.
54 Or, as in the USA, offers corporations a choice as to which jurisdiction's laws and regulations will apply ....

objectives. One of the most characteristic features of German corporations is 'co-determination', the requirement that supervisory boards include a stipulated percentage of employee representatives. The inclusion of employee representatives is specifically intended to prevent corporations from pursuing courses of action that lack employee support; so is the veto that employee representatives are allowed over the appointment of non-employee representatives to the supervisory board. Employee advocates, and proponents of stakeholder theory, applaud such measures as providing protection for employee interests. But by limiting corporations to those ends endorsed by employees, the German legal requirement constitutes an explicit restriction on the corporate ends that shareholders may choose. As will be argued more comprehensively below, in the section on stakeholder theory, the price of such limitations is very high indeed: what is at stake is nothing less than private property and the relationship of agent and principal.

Before considering stakeholder theory, however, it is instructive to review briefly the different ways in which the Japanese model achieves some of the same outcomes as the much praised German model. Like the German system, the Japanese system puts a very high value on consensus, and achieves it by means that impede the attainment of shareholder value. In contrast to the German model, however, the pursuit of shareholder shareholders' ends is not explicitly precluded by Japanese law[55]: setting corporate objectives is within the legal powers of the shareholders of Japanese corporations.

---

55 Though both dividends and profits have been subject to legal restrictions for long periods. 'A cautionary tale' in 'A Survey of Japanese Finance', *The Economist*, 28 June 1997, p. 5.

In many respects, the formal corporate governance mechanisms employed in Japanese corporations resemble those used in Anglo-American jurisdictions; considering how strongly Japanese law, including corporate law, was influenced by the Americans after World War II, this is hardly surprising. The Japanese model of corporate governance might perhaps be regarded as a variant of the Anglo-American model in which the characteristic use of corporate form is not to run a business dedicated to maximising shareholder value, but to advance the interests of a corporate 'family'.[56] Shareholders are typically other corporations in the same corporate grouping[57]; the key corporate objective is maximising the growth of the corporate 'family' via market share.

Theoretically, of course, there is no reason why corporate agents should not be as accountable to shareholders for achieving this corporate objective as they would be for maximising shareholder value. Given the extremely high value the Japanese place on consensus, however, and the traditional Japanese aversion to adversarial confrontations[58], shareholders of Japanese companies have in fact adopted corporate mechanisms that promote harmony rather accountability.

---

56 According to 4A of the official Japanese Corporate Governance Principles, directors bear 'the important responsibility of coordinating the various interests of all the other stakeholders.' Corporate Governance Committee, Corporate Governance Forum of Japan, *Corporate Governance Principles: A Japanese View* (Final Report), 26 May 1998, p. 46;
http://papers.ssrn.com/paper.taf?abstract_id=99032311.

57 On average, two thirds of the shares of leading Japanese companies are held by their business partners. William Dawkins, 'Tradition on a knife-edge', *Financial Times*, 13 March 1997, p. 21.

58 Gillian Tett, 'Gang payoffs cost Japanese companies dear', *Financial Times*, 28 April 1997, p. 4.

Thus, for example, boards in Japanese companies are used to secure commitment to agreed results, not to take decisions or establish control[59]. For achieving that distinctive purpose, their large size[60] and incestuous composition are not an impediment, but a positive advantage. Similarly, because the corporation is regarded as a 'family', there is neither need nor scope for external directors[61]. Reinforcing 'family' solidarity, directors are either managers who are promoted to the board as a sign of approval by their colleagues, or are executives of related firms; shareholders are not expected to challenge board appointments, but to show their approval with a round of applause.[62] When dissidence is socially proscribed, and all participants in a corporation are predisposed to pursue the same objectives, structural mechanisms to hold corporate agents to those objectives may seem dispensable.

That the Japanese consider harmony to be of overwhelming importance does not, however, diminish the value of accountability, or its essential role in corporate governance. The fact that the Japanese model favours other values over accountability may explain why it is preferred by some critics of the Anglo-American system. But it cannot be a reason for advocating it a superior system of corporate governance.

In summary, it is hardly surprising that the German and Japanese models are defective in holding corporations to their owners' objectives: protecting the rights of owners has little or no place in the German and Japanese systems. In line with their cultures, the

---

59 Tricker, *International Corporate Governance, op. cit.*, p. 21.

60 Boards often have 30–40 members. *JJTI, op. cit.*.

61 *Ibid.*, p. 47. For a discussion of the ways in which businesses differ from families, and the dangers of confusing the two, see Sternberg, *JB, op. cit.*, pp. 37–8.

62 Tricker, *International Corporate Governance, op. cit.*, p. 47.

German and Japanese systems are neither designed to protect, nor used for protecting, property rights. The arguments in favour of the Anglo-American system of corporate governance therefore go far beyond whatever economic superiority it may support. A fundamental reason for preferring the Anglo-American system to all the others is that it alone respects the property rights that are so essential for protecting individual liberty.

6   THE DEFECTS OF THE STAKEHOLDER DOCTRINE[1]

So neither Germany nor Japan provides a superior model of corporate governance: both represent inferior, not superior, ways of keeping corporate agents to corporate objectives. Perhaps, as many have suggested, what is needed instead is a stakeholder approach. The stakeholder doctrine[2] has indeed been so widely advocated that it represents a new orthodoxy.[3] Far from being a source of improvements, however, the stakeholder doctrine is fundamentally

---

1   Earlier versions of this section have been published as 'Stakeholder Theory Exposed' in *The Corporate Governance Quarterly* (HK), 2(1), March 1996, pp. 4–18 and *Economic Affairs*, 16(3), summer 1996, pp. 36–8, as 'The Defects of Stakeholder Theory' in *Corporate Governance* 5(1), January 1997, pp. 3–10, as 'Stakeholder Theory: The Defective State It's In', in *Stakeholding and its Critics*, IEA Choice in Welfare No. 36, 1997, pp. 70–85, and as *The Stakeholder Concept: A Mistaken Doctrine*, The Foundation for Business Responsibilities, 1999; http://papers.ssrn.com/paper.taf?abstract_id=263144.

2   Often called 'stakeholder theory'.

3   Stakeholder doctrines have become a staple of management theory and conventional business ethics, and the subject of extensive academic examination. They have been adopted by prominent management groups, and used to inform official policy on directors' duties, takeovers and public pension fund investments.

 In the USA, stakeholder interests have been recognised by law in 38 states; James L. Hanks, 'From the Hustings: The Role of States with Takeover Control Laws', *Mergers & Acquisitions*, 29(2), September/October 1994; quoted in Monks and Minnow, *CG, op. cit.*, p. 38, note 43.

 In Britain, the stakeholder concept was endorsed as early as 1973 by the Watkinson Report on *The responsibilities of the British public company* (Confederation of British Industry Company Affairs Committee, 1973; quoted in Sir Adrian

misguided, incapable of providing better corporate governance, corporate performance or corporate conduct. The stakeholder doctrine is indeed intrinsically incompatible with all substantive corporate objectives, and undermines both private property and accountability.

The development of the stakeholder concept

The term 'stakeholder' is popularly associated with three conflicting doctrines, two commonplace and the other largely incoherent. If taking a stakeholder approach simply means recognising that people are more likely to take an interest in a process when they are materially involved in its outcome, then 'stakeholding' is an important notion, but one that is neither distinctive nor new. Similarly, if 'stakeholding' simply means recognising that a wide variety of interests must ordinarily be taken into account when pursuing organisational objectives, then all that is exceptional about stakeholding is the label; the underlying truth has long been

Cadbury, *The Company Chairman*, 2nd edn, Director Books, 1995, p. 146). Laws requiring its adoption have been advocated by the Confederation of British Industry (*ibid.*) as well as by the Trades Union Congress ('Monks proposes company law reform', *Financial Times*, 18 March 1995). Protection of specific stakeholder interests has been enshrined in at least 44 main UK statutes, in addition to statutory instruments and EU regulations (Confederation of British Industry, *Boards without tiers*, October 1996, p. 23; *EUcsr, op. cit.*). The 'stakeholder economy' was the Labour Party's initial 'defining theme' for the 1997 general election campaign (Robert Peston, 'Votes at stake over vision for economy', *Financial Times*, 11 January 1996, p. 5). The stakeholder doctrine has even been endorsed by the *Financial Times* ('Governance revisited', leader 22 August 1995). And disturbingly, the stakeholder doctrine was one of the 'three pillars' that underpinned the current review of UK company law. It was designated the 'pluralist approach' in the section on the scope of company law; without any label, it continues to underlie proposals for major changes in UK company formation procedures.

recognised and accepted. It is only when force is added to those traditional notions that 'stakeholder theory' denotes something distinctive: the doctrine that organisations should be run for the benefit of, and should be accountable to, all their stakeholders. It is in this last sense, however, that stakeholding has recently become popular.

The meaning of the term 'stakeholder' has itself changed significantly over time. When it was first used as a technical term[4], 'stakeholder' identified those without whom an organisation could not survive, those in whom the organisation had a stake. Now, in contrast, stakeholders are more commonly identified as those who have a stake *in* an organisation. Contemporary usage transforms everyone into a stakeholder, by excluding all criteria of materiality, immediacy and legitimacy: 'A stakeholder in an organization is (by definition) any group or individual who can affect or is affected by the achievement of the organization's objectives.'[5] Given the increasing internationalisation of modern life, and the global connections made possible by improved transportation, telecommunications and computing power, those affected (at least distantly and indirectly) by any given organisation include virtually everyone, everything, everywhere. Terrorists[6] and competitors[7], vegeta-

---

4   In a 1963 internal memorandum at the Stanford Research Institute (now SRI International, Inc.); it referred there to 'those groups without whose support the organisation would cease to exist'. R. Edward Freeman, *Strategic Planning: a Stakeholder Approach*, Pitman Publishing, 1984, pp. 31–2.

5   *Ibid.*, p. 46. This definition is the one adopted by, for example, the Body Shop (Mark Suzman, 'The social audit', *Financial Times*, 24 January 1996, p. 20) and the European Union: 'Stakeholder: an individual, community or organisation that affects, or is affected by, the operations of a company.' (*EUcsr, op. cit.*, Concepts Annex, p. 28).

6   R. Edward Freeman, *Strategic Planning, op. cit.*, p. 53.

7   *Ibid.*, pp. 17, 55.

tion[8] and nameless sea creatures[9], and generations yet unborn[10] are amongst the many groups which are now seriously considered to be business stakeholders.

Like the criterion of being a stakeholder, the main uses of the stakeholder doctrine have also altered radically. Whereas the stakeholder model was originally proposed as a better way of achieving the ends traditionally sought by business corporations, it is now most commonly advocated by those who are hostile to those ends. The most fervent supporters of the stakeholder doctrine are those who seek to do away with business as it has traditionally been understood, and those, notably business managers, who seek to subvert essential features of business accountability. As will be argued below, this reversal is a natural concomitant of the changed meaning of 'stakeholder'.

Before demonstrating that conclusion, however, the many uses of 'stakeholder', 'the stakeholder doctrine' and 'stakeholder theory' make it is necessary to clarify exactly how those terms will be used here. To ensure that the full range of criticisms is covered, 'stakeholders' will be used inclusively, to refer to all those who can affect, or are affected by, an organisation; most of the criticisms would, however, apply even if 'stakeholders' were to refer only to shareowners, employees, suppliers, lenders, customers, and society. 'The stakeholder doctrine' ('stakeholder theory')

---

8   The rainforests ....
9   Those allegedly threatened by the disposal of Brent Spar at the bottom of the ocean.
10   The UK Co-operative Bank explicitly includes both 'past and future generations' in its list of stakeholders; Lucy Kellaway, 'Stakeholders step up for the generation shuffle', *Financial Times*, 17 March 1997, p. 16. Consider as well the future generations, of whatever species, in whose name ecologists protest against various perceived depredations and in favour of sustainability.

is the doctrine that organisations, including corporations and particularly businesses, should be run not to serve the interests of their owners, but for the benefit of all their stakeholders. It is an essential tenet of stakeholder theory that organisations are accountable to all their stakeholders, and that the proper objective of management is to balance stakeholders' competing interests.

The stakeholder doctrine is incompatible with business and all substantive objectives

The first thing to be said against stakeholder theory is that whatever else it may be, it is not a sensible model of, or even compatible with, either business or most other corporate objectives. And that is because the definitive stakeholder aim – balanced benefits for all stakeholders – precludes all objectives which favour particular groups. Business understood as the activity of maximising long-term owner value is automatically ruled out. So are the quite different aims of maximising value-added for customers and improving benefits for employees. The stakeholder doctrine equally precludes organisations from having as their goals housing the homeless, curing the sick, and conducting scientific research. Since all organisations with substantive ends aim at something other than 'balanced stakeholder benefits', they are all ruled out by stakeholder theory. The stakeholder doctrine does not allow for the variety of corporate purposes; according to stakeholder theory, there is only one legitimate organisational objective: balanced stakeholder benefits.

Supporters of stakeholder theory may now object: what they advocate is not dispensing with substantive objectives, but pursuing them while serving the interests of all the stakeholders. Unfortunately, their insistence on multiple accountability makes substantive objectives difficult to sustain.

Consider an organisation that purports to be a business, but attempts to operate in accordance with stakeholder theory. It differs from an ordinary business in several significant ways. First, whereas an ordinary business[11] is accountable to its owners[12], a stakeholder business is supposed to be accountable to all of its stakeholders. This presumably means that the managers, employees and other agents of the stakeholder business are accountable to all of the business's stakeholders instead of just to the owners. But the managers, employees and other agents are themselves stakeholders of the business. The stakeholder doctrine would therefore seem to render them accountable *inter alia* to themselves, without offering any explanation of how such multiple self-accountability is meant to work.

Even more significantly, however, what is the outcome for which the business's agents are accountable to all of its stakeholders? By hypothesis, the objective of the stakeholder business will not be the ordinary business objective. At best it will be the business objective subject to the interests of all the stakeholders. In holding the organisation accountable, however, there is no reason to assume that all the stakeholders will give the business objective the same weight. Indeed, no stakeholder group has any particular incentive to advance the business objective instead of its own interests. Each group may therefore give its own interests

11   Where the business is corporate in form, and thus legally distinct from its owners. In other organisational forms, where the business is legally identified with its owners, it is the business's agents, e.g., employees, managers, etc., that are accountable to the owners.

12   And other parties to which it has rendered itself accountable through (typically) contractual arrangements.

priority over both the business objective and the interests of the other stakeholders: there is nothing in stakeholder theory to stop customers from seeking a free handout, or employees a sinecure.

In such circumstances, it becomes clear why the role of management is reduced to 'balancing stakeholders' benefits', without any reference to achieving substantive objectives. It is because, being accountable to all of the stakeholders, and preoccupied with the need to balance the stakeholders conflicting interests, managements typically have neither occasion nor incentive to pursue substantive objectives. Despite what advocates of the stakeholder doctrine may claim, substantive objectives are systematically undermined by essential features of the stakeholder doctrine.

In the absence of substantive objectives, the meaning and applicability of the stakeholder doctrine depend heavily on what is involved in balancing stakeholder benefits. Unfortunately, that notion does not withstand critical scrutiny.

First, stakeholder theory offers no guidance as to how the appropriate individuals or groups should be selected. Since stakeholders are all those who can affect or are affected by the organisation, the number of people whose benefits need to be taken into account is infinite. For a balance to be struck, however, their numbers must somehow be limited. Even the ostensibly simple category 'employee' leaves many questions open. Are temporary employees to be included in the category, or just permanent staff? Are part-timers to be included on the same basis as full-timers? Does the category of 'employee' include pensioners? Former employees? Probationary trainees? Potential recruits? Some non-arbitrary criterion needs to be found if these questions are to be answered satisfactorily. But stakeholder theory offers none. Furthermore, individuals are often members of more than one stakeholder group. Employees may be shareholders; shareholders may be customers; suppliers may be creditors. In which capacity or capacities are they to be included in the calculation?

Second, even if the stakeholder groups could be identified and restricted to a manageable number, stakeholder theory does not explain what should count as a benefit for the purposes of balancing benefits. Is everything that a stakeholder regards as beneficial to be included in the calculation? And how are the managers to know what stakeholders consider to be benefits? Despite the simplifying and often presumptuous assumptions that are commonly made, even members of the same notional stakeholder constituency may have significantly different views as to what is beneficial. Some employees want higher wages, others want shorter hours; some regard more responsibility as a benefit, others consider it to be a burden. How are stakeholders' divergent perceptions of benefit to be discerned and entered into the balance?

Third, and most fundamentally, even if the relevant benefits could somehow be identified, stakeholder theory provides no guidance as to how the balance is to be struck. Given the divergent interests of the different stakeholder groups, that which benefits one group will often harm another. Higher wages for employees can mean higher prices for customers and/or lower returns for shareholders. Cleaner emissions into the environment may mean harder work for employees and loss of market share for traditional suppliers. What weight is to be given to these conflicting interests? Even within a notional stakeholder group, benefits may well conflict with each other. Higher wages for some employees may require layoffs of others, and money spent on redundancy payments or on pensions is not available for wages. The stakeholder doctrine does not indicate which of these benefits is to be preferred, or how conflicting interests are to be balanced. Are stakeholder interests all strictly equal? Are some more important than others? If so, which are they? And when, and by how much, and why? The stakeholder doctrine gives no clue as to how to rank or reconcile the normally conflicting interests of stakeholders.

It may now be protested that such problems are, nonetheless, routinely resolved in practice. And indeed they are. But the way that they are resolved, is by using the substantive goal of the organisation as a decision criterion. If the purpose of a corporation is to maximise long-term owner value, or to produce the environmentally-friendliest widgets, or to provide employment for the blind, that purpose enables managers to identify which groups need to be considered, and which of their perceived benefits are relevant and legitimate; it indicates how benefits are to be ranked, and how conflicts are to be resolved. The only way that stakeholder theory can be made workable, is to employ the very substantive objectives that it explicitly rejects[13]. Like a parasite, stakeholder theory is viable only so long as its targets withstand its attacks.

The stakeholder doctrine is incompatible with corporate governance

The stakeholder doctrine is as incompatible with good corporate governance as it is with substantive corporate objectives. As indicated above, the key concept in corporate governance is accountability: the accountability of directors to shareholders, and the accountability of corporate employees and other corporate agents to the corporation. The stakeholder doctrine is inimical to them both.

---

13   Or to justify some other principle of allocation.

And this is not surprising. The stakeholder doctrine does, after all, explicitly deny that corporations should be accountable to their owners: it is an essential principle of stakeholder theory that corporations should be equally accountable to *all* their stakeholders. This core doctrine is, however, not only wholly unjustified, but unworkable. An organisation that is accountable to everyone, is actually accountable to no one: accountability that is diffuse, is effectively non-existent. Multiple accountability can only function if everyone involved accepts a clear common purpose. But that is what stakeholder theory conspicuously rejects.

Furthermore, stakeholder theory provides no effective standard against which corporate agents can be judged. Balancing stakeholder interests is an ill-defined notion, which cannot serve as an objective performance measure; managers responsible for interpreting as well as implementing it are effectively left free to pursue their own arbitrary ends. Accordingly, stakeholder theory gives full rein to arrogant and unresponsive managements, and to extravagance in respect of salaries, perks and premises. The stakeholder doctrine licenses resistance to takeover bids that would benefit shareholders, and permits the pursuit of empire-building acquisitions that make little business sense. The stakeholder doctrine indulges exploitation by lenders, and inferior performance by employees and suppliers. So despite the pious hopes which are so often attached to stakeholder theory, it is unlikely to improve either corporate performance or corporate governance.

But the prognosis is even worse. The stakeholder doctrine is not only prone to impair corporate governance: it is *bound* to do so. Most conditions of employment include an at least nominal commitment to furthering the employer's purposes. The stakeholder doctrine, however, requires managers to ignore those purposes, and balance stakeholder interests instead. Inciting betrayal of trust is a particularly ironic feature in a theory supposed to promote better conduct.

The stakeholder doctrine of accountability is unjustified

So stakeholder theory cannot serve as a useful model of corporate governance in any traditional sense; it destroys, rather than supports, conventional corporate accountability. Can stakeholder theory justify its alternative doctrine, that corporations, and more generally organisations, should be accountable to all their stakeholders ... whatever that might mean?

The first thing to note is that although this precept is both essential to stakeholder theory and highly contentious, attempts are seldom made to justify it. Most stakeholder theorists proceed without argument from the undeniable fact that organisations are affected by and affect certain factors, to the unjustified conclusion that organisations should be accountable to them. But that cannot be right. Organisations are affected by gravity and affect employment levels, but they are not, and logically could not be, held to account by them. Natural forces and economic statistics are not the sorts of things that can hold agents to account. Equally, organisations affect and are affected by burglars and terrorists and saboteurs, but could not sensibly be accountable to them. That an organisation must take many factors into account, does not give them any right to hold it to account. Nor does the fact that various groups are affected by an organisation give them any right to control it. If stakeholder theorists are to maintain their claim that organisations are accountable to all their stakeholders, some convincing argument is needed.

The residual risk argument

One argument that is sometimes presented in support of accountability to all stakeholders relies on the presence of firm-specific skills or products. Firm-specific skills and products are considered risky, because they cannot be easily transferred without loss of value; they are difficult to protect contractually because, being long term, they are liable to contingencies which cannot all be predicted or managed in advance. By developing them, it is alleged, stakeholders become exposed to the firm's residual risk, which was traditionally thought to attach only to owners. But having exposed themselves to that residual risk, stakeholders should, it is maintained, have the right to hold the company accountable in order to protect their investments.

The first thing to be noted about this argument is that it could only justify accountability to all stakeholders – which is what is required for the stakeholder doctrine – if all stakeholders made firm-specific investments. But most jobs and products are far from firm-specific: they are, instead, readily transferable. Being a secretary or an accountant is not something that can be done only in one firm; reading a script in a call-centre does not require having, or developing, skills that are useful only in one company. Equally, most manufacuturers still produce products that have many applications and purchasers.

Second, stakeholders' firm-specific commitments are seldom as they are portrayed in the argument. Even when skills and products have firm-specific elements, the main skills and products involved are still transferable. Selling should involve knowing something specific about the product or service sold, but the skill of selling, and the skill of learning about products or services, can be usefully employed in all sorts of employments. Salesmen are renowned for their ability to shift successfully from one company to another; so are computer programmers. No matter how idiosyncratic or deeply ingrained a company's culture, any job done that genuinely adds value is likely to be based on transferable skills. Similarly, products that add value are frequently based on transferable processes. Modern computerised production techniques are designed precisely to permit producing specialised, customer-specific outputs with minimal marginal investment or effort.

Moreover, skills and products that appear to be significantly firm-specific may be more, not less, valuable for that very reason. The knowledge that employees gain when working for firms that provide specialist products or services is often highly prized in the marketplace. Its value is recognised in contracts of employment that require a period of 'gardening leave' before knowledgeable employees can accept jobs with competitors; such contracts also typically restrict specialists' permission to take colleagues with them when they move to competing firms. Similarly, products or services designed for use by one firm, are often actively sought by others; they are expected to increase the provider's market value as it exploits a new market niche.

Third, even in the atypical cases when stakeholders' skills or products are valuable and genuinely firm-specific, and are not easily usable elsewhere, the right conclusion is not that the firm should be accountable to those stakeholders as stakeholders, or that such stakeholders should be granted some of the privileges of shareholders. The correct response is instead recognising that, in making equity-like investments, and bearing equity-like residual risks, such stakeholders deserve actually to be shareholders. And this is ordinarily what happens. It is a commonplace that pioneers in high technology firms are remunerated with shares in those firms. Equally, when companies need to have long-standing and complex relations with one another, they typically cement those relationships by exchanging equity, or by both taking equity in a specially created joint venture. Shares can be earned in kind – by contributing skills or products or assets – as well as paid for in cash. But it is only shareholders to whom accountability is legitimately due.

The performance argument

A variation on the risk argument, is the performance argument, which maintains that accountability to stakeholders is necessary to achieve optimum performance. One form asserts that unless strong relationships of trust are fostered, stakeholders are unlikely to commit the time and resources required to develop firm-specific skills and products that may be needed for business success. Another popular form suggests that the best way to achieve business success is not to concentrate narrowly on financial outcomes, but to strive instead to delight customers, to empower employees, to form lasting partnerships with suppliers, etc.

To the extent that such strategies enhance motivation or improve quality or build trust, they may well be justified as effective means for achieving the business end, and provide support for the uncontroversial functional relationship approach to stakeholding. But the practical success of stakeholder-oriented strategies neither does nor can justify the doctrine under review here, that organisations should be accountable to all their stakeholders. Establishing accountability to all stakeholders requires showing that they have legitimate authority over an organisation, not that they are functionally useful to it. As the property of its owners, a corporation is properly accountable only to them.[14]

The obligation argument

Accountability to stakeholders is sometimes thought to result from the fact that organisations have obligations to stakeholders. But the conclusion is mistaken. The individuals or groups to whom one is accountable for fulfilling an obligation are not necessarily the ones to whom the obligation is owed: one can be accountable to A for fulfilling an obligation to B. Parents, for example, have an obligation to care for their infant children, but they are normally answerable to other adults, not to their infants, for doing so. Equally, an obligation not to poison the atmosphere does not and could not render anyone accountable to the atmosphere. Furthermore, organisations only have obligations to some stakeholders. Organisations incur obligations by entering into specific, typically contractual, relationships: it is those contractual relationships, not being a stakeholder, that produce the obligations. The fact that organisations do ordinarily have obligations to some of their stakeholders therefore cannot justify the claim that the organisations are accountable to all of their stakeholders.

---

14 Though it may render itself accountable to other parties through contractual arrangements. The fact that business can be held to account by government is a function of the coercive power of government, not its notional role as stakeholder. The extent to which government has any *right* to control business in this way is a quite separate matter, and is a key issue of political philosophy.

Treating stakeholders as ends

Another argument alleges that organisations should be accountable to all their stakeholders, because otherwise those stakeholders would be treated merely as means to others' ends. One reason that this is deemed to be wrong, is that treating stakeholders as means is alleged to be a less effective way of achieving substantive objectives. This may sometimes be true, but as already argued, performance is irrelevant to justifying accountability.

More fundamentally, it is sometimes claimed that treating stakeholders as means to others' ends is morally wrong. Although commonly associated with Kantian philosophy[15], that assertion is itself unjustified. To the extent that stakeholders include environmental features and abstract groupings, the dictum makes no sense: even for Kant, it is only persons – rational moral agents – who must be treated as ends in themselves. Moreover, treating persons as ends in themselves merely means respecting their moral agency. That neither precludes persons' being instrumental in serving others' ends, nor requires accountability to them.

Far from supporting stakeholder theory, the requirement to treat persons as ends provides a strong argument against it. Respecting persons as moral agents requires allowing persons to choose their own ends. But this is what the stakeholder doctrine conspicuously fails to do. Instead of respecting the ends freely chosen by consenting moral agents, stakeholder theory systematically and forcibly overrides them, in favour of balancing stakeholder benefits. 'Treating persons as ends' effectively

---

15   Which even when properly understood cannot sustain a viable ethical theory …; see, e.g., Alasdair MacIntyre, *After Virtue: a study in ethical theory*, Duckworth, 1981.

precludes stakeholder theory; it certainly cannot justify the stakeholder doctrine of accountability to all stakeholders.

The parallel with government[16]

Another unsuccessful argument for accountability to all stakeholders comes from confusing corporate governance with government. Democratic governments, it is alleged, are accountable to their citizens; citizens are equal under the law, and are entitled to representation and a vote. Regarding stakeholders in an organisation as citizens of that organisation, some commentators have assumed that stakeholders have comparable rights.

This conclusion is unfounded for several reasons. First, the argument overlooks the special nature of government: government is different from all other organisations because of its monopoly on the legitimate use of physical violence[17]. It is because government has the power forcibly to deprive the governed of their lives[18], liberty and property, that it is vital for those[19] subject to its power to have a say in how that power is used.

Comparable accountability is neither required nor justified in non-governmental organisations. Unlike government, ordinary organisations cannot legally use force to compel anyone to do anything; they cannot even enforce their own contracts without recourse to the courts. Since organisations have no coercive power, there is no need to hold them accountable for its use.

---

16 This section draws heavily on Sternberg, *JB, op. cit.*, pp. 39–40, 50.
17 Although individuals typically retain the right to self-defence.
18 By conscription into the armed forces, and in some jurisdictions through capital punishment.
19 To the extent that they are competent adults who have not forfeited their rights.

Those who do not wish to comply with an organisation's decision or policy can simply leave[20]; in ordinary organisations, unlike in government, participants can ordinarily vote with their feet.[21] The parallel with government thus fails at the outset: non-governmental organisations are too different from governments for the comparison to be valid.

Even if the parallel could be sustained, however, the stakeholder theorists' conclusion still would not follow: contrary to the argument's assumption, even democratic governments are not accountable to all their citizens. Those who have been certified insane or who are underage or are convicted felons typically may not vote. Until quite recently youths aged 18 to 21 lacked the franchise.

Still less are governments accountable to all their stakeholders. Foreigners affect and are affected by governmental actions, but have no say in controlling them; foreign visitors, even long-term foreign residents, suffer taxation without representation. Corporations are clearly affected by and affect government, but cannot vote, even though they are domestic legal persons.

The parallel with government therefore provides no support for the conclusion that organisations should be accountable to all their stakeholders. Even as democratic governments are accountable only to some of their citizens – to sane, non-felonious adults – organisations are properly accountable only to some of their stakeholders – for corporations, to the shareholders and those

---

20 Subject, of course, to fulfilling any contractual commitments they might have undertaken.

21 Stakeholders who object to the effects of a corporation's policies can also withhold their custom and financial support, and direct it to the corporation's competitors. See the discussion of 'conscientious stakeholding' in the section 'As the key to "social responsibility"' below in this chapter (pp.152–4).

with whom the corporation has entered into specific contractual agreements. So the parallel with government cannot sustain the stakeholder theorists' claim.

The social contract/licence to operate argument

Another defence that stakeholder theorists sometimes offer for their position is a form of 'social contract' or 'licence to operate' argument. According to this line of reasoning, organisations are accountable to all their stakeholders because organisations use society's resources and enjoy special privileges from society.[22] In exchange for society's consenting to provide the resources and privileges that organisations need to exist, and granting them a 'licence to operate', organisations become accountable to society. Though superficially plausible, this argument is based on confusions about the nature of both consent and of accountability; it, too, does not support the stakeholder theorists' conclusion.

Consent normally means one of two things: tacit agreement or formal authorisation. In the sense of tacit agreement, it is certainly true that organisations require the consent of society. Consider a business. Unless members of society acting as investors agree to provide capital, unless members of society acting as employees

---

22   Another version claims that stakeholder theory would be the outcome if individuals operating behind a Rawlsian 'veil of ignorance' were to enter into a social contract; R. Edward Freeman and William M. Evans, 'Corporate Governance: A Stakeholder Interpretation', *Journal of Behavioral Economics*, Vol. 19, 1990, pp. 337–59. Building upon the flawed Rawlsian base, and incorporating additional errors, the claim does not succeed. For a Rawlsian critique of the argument, see James W. Child and Alexei M. Marcoux, 'Freeman and Evans: Stakeholder Theory in the Original Position', *Business Ethics Quarterly*, 9(2), April 1999, pp. 207–21.

agree to provide labour, unless members of society acting as suppliers agree to provide materials, etc., businesses cannot operate. And unless members of society acting as customers agree to buy their products and services, businesses cannot survive.

But though organisations certainly depend on the tacit agreement – indeed the willing cooperation – of the members of society, that does not give society at large any right to hold them to account. Being affected by a group, even needing to be functionally responsive to a group, is quite different from being accountable to that group. Organisations must indeed take various groups into account. But they are answerable to those groups only insofar as the law or specific contractual arrangements have made them so.[23] Members of society can withdraw their cooperation, but they have no general authority to hold organisations to account.

Perhaps, then, the 'social contract' argument for accountability to all stakeholders relies on the notion of consent as formal permission. On the face of it, this is less plausible. It is a defining characteristic of free societies that whatever is not expressly prohibited is allowed, and that strict limits apply as to what may be officially prohibited. Since individuals already possess all the powers they need to run organisations, consent in the sense of formal permission is seldom necessary: most businesses require no special licence to operate.

There are some cases, of course, in which formal permissions are required to establish or operate organisations, especially when organisations enjoy special privileges. To constitute an English corporation, for example, and enjoy separate legal existence and limited liability for shareholders, it is necessary to file

---

23 See Sternberg, *JB, op. cit.*, especially pp. 41–2.

a Memorandum and Articles of Association with the Registrar of Companies, and comply with the requirements of the Companies Acts.

When such formal permissions are needed, however, the privileges conceded and the considerations expected are both explicitly stipulated. So are the procedures for obtaining them: typically, designated undertakings must be submitted to designated authorities, often accompanied by the payment of designated fees. The obligations involved are specific, and specific to the kind of organisation: to compensate for their special privileges, corporations must pay corporation taxes. Contrary to the stakeholder theorists' claim, even organisations that require formal authorisation have no general obligation to society to which they can be held accountable by all stakeholders. The claim to such accountability is no more justified by formal permission than it is by tacit agreement.

On what, then, is the stakeholder theorists' argument based? The core of their argument is actually very simple: organisations are liable to control by society because they need society's permission to operate. Since organisations already exist, and do so routinely, however, this statement looks rather like a threat: organisations must submit themselves to society's requirements, because otherwise society will retract its consent. Stakeholder theorists seem to be relying on what looks very like extortion: agreeing not to inflict harm in exchange for appeasement is not entering into a social contract, but running a protection racket.

The undeniable fact that some groups may have power over an organisation – even the power to destroy that organisation – does not, and cannot, give those groups legitimate authority over the organisation, or the right to hold it to account. The fact that muggers may kill you if you do not surrender your money, does not give muggers the right to your money or to your life; it simply means that they are capable of theft and murder. Claims to justify accountability require demonstrations of entitlement, not displays of raw power.

The stakeholder doctrine undermines private property, agency and wealth

So the stakeholder theorists have not been able to justify their claim that organisations should be accountable to all their stakeholders. Since stakeholder theory is so widely accepted even without justification, however, it is important to recognise just how serious its implications are. In particular, it is essential to understand that stakeholder theory undermines two of the most fundamental features that characterise modern society: private property and the duties that agents owe to principals.

The stakeholder doctrine undermines private property, because it denies owners the right to determine how their property will be used. Insofar as assets are held or utilised by organisations, stakeholder theory stipulates that those assets should be used for the balanced benefit of all stakeholders. The owners of those assets are thereby prevented from devoting their property unequivocally to the ends of their choice, whether those ends are maximising owner value, housing the homeless or finding a cure for cancer. It may be argued that since stakeholder theory concerns only organisational property, this is a small infringement. But since most property is manufactured, financed, distributed or otherwise processed through organisations, it would leave almost no property subject to owner control.

Stakeholder theorists sometimes attempt to justify curtailing property rights by indicating that property rights are seldom absolute. But the fact that some limitations may apply, is not an argument for conceding others: the abolition of slavery does not justify the confiscation of land. As importantly, the fact that property rights may be weakly enforced, provides no justification for violating them. An overworked or lazy police force may make theft easier to accomplish; it does not give robbers the right to one's goods. Despite what stakeholder theorists suggest, the fact that shareholders are sometimes unwilling or unable actively to protect their interests, does not entitle other stakeholders to commandeer corporate property.

The stakeholder doctrine also denies the duty that agents owe to principals. Whenever one entrusts one's assets or affairs to another, the agent/ principal relationship is invoked. It arises in respect of corporate directors and corporate managers; it also exists in every case of employment, whatever the organisational form of the employer. Agents' duty to principals is also central to the conduct of civil servants and armies, investment managers and lawyers, school teachers and motor mechanics. The stakeholder doctrine makes this critical relationship unworkable, by denying that agents have any particular duty to their principals. According to stakeholder theory, organisational agents are equally accountable to all stakeholders ... and thus to no one.

Why, then, is stakeholder theory so popular? One reason is that its implications are seldom recognised. Another is that stakeholder theory appears to offer a free lunch; it attracts those who would like to enjoy the benefits of business without the discipline of business. It particularly appeals to those with much to gain from undermining accountability, including politicians and the business managers who would like to have the power and prestige and perks of office without the concomitant responsibilities. Stakeholder doctrine also appeals to the promoters of worthy 'causes', who believe they would be the beneficiaries if business profits were diverted from business owners.

But they are mistaken: nothing comes from nothing. The wealth that they want from business will not be available if the essential business objective of maximising long-term owner value is forsaken, and investors are not allowed to reap the benefits of their investments. In the spurious expectation of achieving vaguely 'nicer' business behaviour, the stakeholder approach would sacrifice not only property rights and accountability, but also the wealth-creating capabilities of business strictly understood.

Implications for public policy

Given the pervasive importance of agent/principal relationships, and the central role of private property in enabling economic activity and political liberty, neither should be surrendered without very good cause. The stakeholder doctrine should therefore be steadfastly resisted in all its manifestations. Corporate mission statements and political rhetoric promoting stakeholder theory may seem innocuous, but they are expressions of a deeply dangerous doctrine.

The stakeholder doctrine is especially pernicious when it is invoked by politicians. One of its most prominent uses is to shift the cost of government regulation from the public to the private sector, and especially to business. Worse still, it does so in a way that allows governments to claim that they have not increased taxes. By (falsely) declaring that, for example, businesses have automatic obligations not just to their owners but to their employees and their customers, to the community and the environment, governments attempt to justify forcing businesses to pay for general public policies. But however commonplace it may be for governments to regulate business, it is hardly just that the cost of government policies intended to benefit everyone should be borne exclusively or disproportionately by business.

The application of stakeholder theory in politics is not just expensive, but ominous. When used by politicians, the stakeholder doctrine is normally a way of presenting old authoritarian and collectivist ambitions in a new guise.[24] Because the public failure of command economies has made the invocation of traditional collectivist slogans largely unacceptable, proponents of *dirigiste* government have had to find a new vocabulary. One of the most popular substitutes is the rhetoric of the 'pluralist' or 'inclusive' stakeholder society.[25] State-imposed controls that were once proclaimed in the name of socialism, or as serving the 'common good', are now often rationalised with the stakeholder doctrine.

The stakeholder doctrine is well suited to serving authoritarian and collectivist political ends. Its nominal association with unobjectionable doctrines lends it a superficial plausibility; its apparent generosity encourages people to accept it uncritically. And its central features – the broad meaning of 'stakeholder', the inability of 'balanced stakeholder interests' to provide an objective criterion

---

24 Be they socialist or fascist .... In continental Europe, stakeholding has long been associated with the notion of *gemeinschaft*. For some of the fascist antecedents of the stakeholder doctrine, see Joseph F. Johnston, *No Man Can Serve Two Masters: Shareholders vs Stakeholders in the Governance of Companies*, Research Report 25, The Social Affairs Unit, 1998, pp. 8–9.

25 Which has long been associated with the 'social market' doctrine of Germany.

of action, the stakeholder doctrine's radical undermining of accountability – mean that almost any kind of state intervention, no matter however intrusive or restrictive, can be defended in terms of stakeholder theory. Furthermore, by undermining private property, the stakeholder doctrine also reduces the ability of those subject to authoritarian government to protect their liberties. The stakeholder doctrine is as much a threat to individual freedom as it is to economic activity, and should be firmly resisted.

Conclusion: the appropriate use of the stakeholder concept

So stakeholder theory is both misguided and mistaken. But this does not mean that there is no legitimate use for the concept of stakeholder. There are indeed two distinct ways in which the concept can be detached from the pernicious stakeholder doctrine and valuably employed.

As a convenient label

First, it is useful as a label. Even – indeed especially – in its broadest interpretation, 'stakeholder' serves as an extremely convenient collective noun for the various groups and individuals that organisations have always needed to take into account when pursuing their substantive objectives. Stakeholders need to be considered both to improve organisations' chances of achieving their objectives, and to ensure that their conduct is ethical.

Consider the business corporation. Although its responsibilities to stakeholders are limited to those created by law and specific agreements, a business cannot afford to ignore any stakeholder concern that might affect its ability to generate long-term owner value. In order to operate, the business must secure the willing co-operation of diverse groups of people. It must therefore consider the preferences not just of shareholders, but of employees and customers, of suppliers and lenders, of regulators and environmental activists. Equally, to be ethical, a business corporation must treat all its stakeholders ethically. Ethical treatment does not, however, mean equating all stakeholders' interests with those of the shareholders; it simply means treating all stakeholders with 'distributive justice' and 'ordinary decency'.[26]

As the key to 'social responsibility'[27]

In addition to being a useful label for all those individuals and groups which have to be taken into account, 'stakeholder' can also help to illuminate the proper meaning of 'social responsibility'.

Most conventional calls for social responsibility rely on some form of the stakeholder doctrine. They typically seek to subjugate constitutional corporate objectives[28] to the interests of various stakeholder groups, to whom they claim that corporations should be automatically accountable. The connection between conventional 'social responsibility' and the stakeholder doctrine is made explicit in the increasingly commonplace concept of the 'triple bottom line'. It contends that organisations should be broadly accountable not just for their economic performance (or more generally, for the achievement of their traditional objectives), but also for their social and environmental effects. In such an organisation,

---

26 See Chapter 3 above.
27 See also Chapter 3 above.
28 And more generally, all organisational objectives.

the task of management is to balance those economic, social and environmental outcomes. As argued above, however, such notions of multiple accountability suffer from fatal defects: the incoherent stakeholder doctrine cannot be the basis for a coherent notion of 'social responsibility'.

There is a way, however, in which 'stakeholder' as a label can be helpful. Consider the corporation again. Although only share-holders have the right to change a corporation's constitutional objectives, everyone can influence corporate conduct. By choos-ing whether or not, and to what extent, to support particular companies with their investment or custom or labour, everyone can contribute to the operating conditions that critically affect corporate decisions. If, therefore, individuals have views as to how corporate activities should be conducted, they should ensure that their individual choices accurately reflect those views .... When each potential stakeholder – otherwise known as every member of society – acts conscientiously in his personal capacity, and strate-gically bestows or withholds his economic and other support on the basis of his moral values, then the operation of market forces will automatically lead corporations to reflect those values. It is as such 'conscientious stakeholding' that social responsibility is properly understood.[29] To the extent that the term 'stakeholder' helps remind people of their individual responsibilities to act con-scientiously, it can serve a second valuable function.

In summary, then, the stakeholder doctrine is either anodyne or incoherent. If it simply highlights the importance of taking stakeholder preferences into account, it is true but hardly new. If,

---

29   For a full discussion of social responsibility see Sternberg, *JB, op. cit.*, Chapter 10, pp. 254–61.

instead, the stakeholder doctrine is something distinctive, it refers to demands that organisations be run for the balanced benefit of all their stakeholders, and that they be accountable to all their stakeholders. In that form, the stakeholder doctrine is incompatible with business and all substantive objectives, and undermines accountability and property rights; it subverts the duty of agents to principals, and the wealth-creating capabilities of business strictly understood. The stakeholder doctrine should, therefore, be firmly resisted.

7 REGULATION, LEGISLATION: SUBSTANTIAL COSTS WITHOUT CORRESPONDING BENEFITS

Notwithstanding the evident superiority of the Anglo-American system of corporate governance over both the German and Japanese alternatives and the stakeholder doctrine, it has often been suggested that the Anglo-American system could be improved through government regulation. Such suggestions have gained force post-Enron, and have led to ambitious regulatory programmes not just in North America, but in Britain, Europe and the Far East.

Attempts to regulate corporate governance are, however, seriously misguided, and reflect a failure to understand its essential nature. The purpose of corporate governance is to ensure that corporations achieve the objectives of their shareholders. Consequently, attempts to restrict shareholder choices through government action are, at best, counterproductive. At worst, they are destructive of both corporate effectiveness and individual liberty.

It is important to differentiate between corporate governance measures that might sensibly be favoured, or even recommended, as general ways of increasing accountability to shareholders, and things that should be made mandatory via legislation or regulation. Not everything that is desirable can or should be compulsory. Many proposals that merit serious consideration by particular shareholders and corporations would nevertheless be wholly inappropriate as mandatory requirements.

Stakeholder regulation

One particularly dangerous sort of regulation is that which attempts to enforce the pernicious stakeholder doctrine. Unfortunately, such laws continue to be widely advocated[1]. They are often presented as ways of promoting corporate 'social responsibility'; increasingly, they use the vocabulary of the 'triple bottom line'. But in whatever guise they appear, they should be firmly resisted. As Friedrich Hayek has pointed out,

> ... once the management of a big enterprise is regarded as not only entitled but obliged to consider in its decisions whatever is regarded as the public or social interest, or to support good causes and generally to act for the public benefit, it gains indeed an uncontrollable power – a power which could not long be left in the hands of private managers but would inevitably be made the subject of increased public control.[2]

Given the practical and theoretical inadequacies of the stakeholder doctrine, and the enormity of its implications, laws to enforce it are a path to unlimited, unconstrained government power.

Even in the absence of explicit 'stakeholder legislation', many jurisdictions already enforce the interests of stakeholders at the expense of shareholders: they have laws and regulations specifying employment practices, health and safety provisions, environmental protection, consumer protection, planning restrictions, etc.. To the extent that such restrictions limit the ways that corporations can frame or pursue their corporate objectives, they make it less likely that corporations will be able to attract shareholders. And

---

1   See Chapter 6 above, note 3.
2   *Law, Legislation, and Liberty*: Volume 3, *The Political Order of a Free People*, University of Chicago Press, 1979, p. 82.

by restricting corporations' ability to maximise long-term owner value, they jeopardise the future of business corporations.

'Functional' regulation

'Functional' regulation to correct 'functional' deficiencies in corporate governance might nevertheless seem like a good idea. Especially post-Enron, most jurisdictions have sought to increase the scope of their regulatory control. The hope is presumably that corporate governance would be improved if 'best practice' were defined in law, and all companies were compelled by law to adopt it. But even this would be a mistake.

First, what advocates of regulation define as 'best practice' frequently has little to do with corporate governance. The reforms they recommend often do not relate to making corporations more accountable for achieving the corporate objectives chosen by their shareholders. Instead, their reforms would force corporations to pursue specific and highly questionable social objectives.

Second, regulation is unnecessary: the chief wrongs involved in the recent scandals were already illegal. Unfortunately, however, like ignorance and risk, dishonesty cannot be eliminated by fiat. Regulation is also largely ineffective against the other major sources of defective corporate governance, which include conflicts of interest, asymmetry of information, and inadequate incentives for monitoring. VERY GOOD

Finally, and more fundamentally, regulation normally produces more harm than good. Indeed, regulation is typically part of the problem, not the solution. Interestingly, the worst scandals have been in industries that have traditionally been heavily regulated: energy, telecoms, defence. Regulators notoriously tend to be

Worse Scandals in markets with regulation

captured by the industries they are meant to regulate. Moreover, the pronouncements of governments and regulators are at least as untrustworthy as those of the groups that they supervise. Consider the state of social security accounts in both the UK and the US[3], and the accounts of the EU[4].

Regulation is necessarily inflexible. But because the purpose of corporate governance is to ensure that the specific objectives of individual corporations are achieved, different mechanisms will be most suitable depending on each corporation's history, size, industry, jurisdiction and shareholder composition. The degree and sort of accountability wanted will appropriately reflect the particular circumstances of each set of shareholders and their organisation. The single size permitted by inflexible regulation will emphatically not fit all.[5]

All regulation imposes substantial costs, in terms of both funds[6] and freedoms: even disclosure is not costless. And all regulations have consequences that are unintended, damaging and difficult to correct.[7] Laws made in response to perceived crises and

---

3 Andrew G. Biggs, 'Don't "Enron" Social Security? It Already Is', Cato Institute, 8 April 2002.

4 For the ninth consecutive year the European Court of Auditors has refused to certify the EU accounts, citing 'significant errors in terms of legality and regularity'. 'Europe on the fiddle', *The Times*, 19 November 2003, p. 21.

5 Care is needed to avoid 'regulatory creep'. Though the 'comply or explain' regime of the Cadbury, Greenbury, Hampel and Higgs reports is ostensibly not coercive, it could easily become *de facto* regulation.

6 For Sarbanes-Oxley Section 404 alone, the cost of initial compliance by Fortune-1000 companies has been estimated to be $2.5 billion; Cath Everett, 'Vie to Comply', *Financial Director*, 1 June 2003, p. 18. The cost of complying with the Higgs recommendations has been estimated to be *c.* £200 million; Richard Donkin, 'Boardroom power and a Godfather factor', *Financial Times*, 15 May 2003, p. 9.

7 Even the Federal Reserve Bank now reportedly regrets the Glass-Steagall Act; aimed at protecting depositors, it balkanised the US financial services industry

hard cases are notoriously defective. The general rule, that ' ... anybody whom a mandate is intended to help is likely to suffer disproportionately from the cost of providing it'[8] is certainly true of attempts to compel better corporate governance. In formalising and clarifying unwritten guidelines, regulation typically lowers standards; compliance no longer requires a margin of safety, but can be obtained by satisfying the letter of the law.[9]

Finally, regulation typically imposes 'benefits' that the ostensible beneficiaries may well not want ... and it adds injury to paternalistic insult by making them pay for it. Regulation specifically intended to protect investors' interests positively impairs those interests by reducing the opportunities for investment, and by making investment more rigid and expensive than it would otherwise be. Regulation to penalise short-term capital gains, discourage dividend distribution or impede takeovers would most likely lead to reduced market liquidity, a higher cost of capital and lower economic efficiency.

---

for nearly six decades. Gerard Baker and Alan Beattie, 'Unstoppable reform', *Financial Times*, 25 July 2002, p. 16. See also Chapter 4 above, *passim*.

8   'Tomorrow's economic argument', *The Economist*, 27 July 1996, p. 21.

9   The three year period that the Greenbury Committee recommended as the minimum period for assessing directors' performance promptly became the maximum ...; John Plender, 'Hampel's rotten boroughs', *Financial Times*, 6 August 1997, p. 18. And whereas UK executives elevated to the board had formerly been known to reduce their contracts to less than twelve months, to avoid disclosure of their remuneration, since the Combined Code's recommendation of a one year maximum for directors' notice or contract periods, one year has become the industry norm; Jean Eaglesham, 'Industry greets "very open" nature of study FAT CAT SALARIES', *Financial Times*, 4 June 2003, p. 3.

Unintended consequences: restricted information

In addition to imposing direct and indirect economic costs[10], regulation can have dangerous unintended consequences. Consider UK and EU regulation against insider trading, for example: intended to provide non-insiders with a level playing field, it has instead created a minefield. Because trading on the basis of 'material unpublished, price-sensitive information possessed as a result of one's employment, profession or duties' constitutes a criminal offence in the UK[11], investors who want to be free to trade must be careful to avoid becoming contaminated with inside information. They are therefore deterred from seeking information that may be necessary for properly monitoring their companies' performance.[12] They are also provided with less information, because companies must be careful to avoid supplying it on a preferential basis. Regulation designed to protect shareholders as investors, has had the effect of harming shareholders as owners; its unintended consequence is to make active corporate governance more hazardous.

Government intervention to protect investors has also reduced the amount of investment information available to them in other ways. In the US, companies are constrained from discussing their prospects in securities prospectuses, lest investors be led astray

10 It is noteworthy that UK regulatory protection of investors is so elaborate and expensive, that the Labour government had to exempt its own proposed 'stakeholder pensions' from it in order to keep their costs acceptably low. Barry Riley, 'Ostriches in on the act', *Financial Times*, 18 April 1998, *Money*, p. I.

11 See the UK Criminal Justice Act 1994 and the EU Insider Dealing Directive 1989.

12 Few organisations can afford to emulate the Prudential Corporation, which has established a 'Chinese wall' separating the Chairman of Prudential Portfolio Managers, who is available for consultation on corporate governance matters, from the fund managers. *Financial Times*, 30 January 1997: William Lewis and Martin Dickenson, 'Pru offers strategy talks with its portfolio', p. 1, and 'Champion of the Chinese Wall', p. 16; Lex: Fund management, p. 20.

by exaggerated claims. Competition, innovation and quality in securities' rating is restricted, because most fund managers are required to use ratings provided by the three 'nationally recognised statistical ratings organisations' ('NRSRO's) designated by the (US) Securities and Exchange Commission[13]; those agencies get paid regardless of the quality of their analysis. It is noteworthy that the designated agencies were no better than the integrated investment banks at warning investors of potential losses from Enron.[14] Nevertheless, post-Enron, regulators have attempted to regulate the provision of research by investment banks. The restrictions imposed to decrease conflicts of interest are, however, more likely to decrease still further the amount of information available. The research departments of the major investment banks have already reduced – typically only to three – the categories used to rate companies[15].

The UK Takeover Code also makes corporate governance more difficult. The Code requires investors acquiring shareholdings over a stipulated size to bid for the entire company; its objective is to protect the interests of minority shareholders. The unintended consequence, however, is that investors may be dissuaded from taking stakes large enough to make a difference to corporate governance, lest doing so trigger the requirement to buy the whole firm. Once again, regulation designed to protect shareholders has had the effect of making it harder for them to act as owners.

And there is much other regulation that has had the effect.

---

13 Standard & Poor's, Moody's and Fitch; Jamie Felix, 'Scores are often junk, say critics', *Financial Times*, 8 March 2003, Section: *FT Money*, p. 5.

14 Vincent Boland, 'The final arbiters of Wall Street: Rating agencies', *Inside Track*, *Financial Times*, 23 July 2002, p. 12.

15 Zarina Rijnen, 'Wall Street sees sharp rise in "sell" recommendations by analysts', *Financial Times*, 12 November 2002, p. 28.

intended or otherwise, of impeding good corporate governance. Consider the US, for example. The Federal Employees' Retirement System Act of 1986 ('FERSA') quite properly seeks to prevent government officials from controlling industry. But it does so by prohibiting the world's largest pension fund from directly exercising voting rights in respect of any its shares.[16] Equally, regulation that requires mutual funds and insurance company investments to be diversified, with a view to making them safer, effectively precludes[17] their taking large enough stakes for long enough to allow the 'relationship investing' advocated by so many corporate governance commentators. And California Proposition 211, intended to improve corporate governance by making directors more accountable, could easily have made them unavailable[18].

Unintended consequences: moral hazards

An especially damaging kind of unintended consequence occurs when the rules provide a positive incentive to do the wrong thing; they then constitute a 'moral hazard'. Although the term is commonly associated with organisations' internal rules, particularly improperly structured performance-related pay schemes, the moral hazards of regulation have led to some of the most costly and dramatic corporate scandals of the last decades; the US sav-

---

16 Monks and Minnow, *PA, op. cit.*, p. 220. The votes are now exercised by the administrator appointed by the trustees.

17 *Ibid.*, pp. 201, 207.

18 211 would have enabled shareholders to sue company directors personally if the share prices of their companies fell suddenly for any reason, regardless of whether the falls reflected actions of the company; Christopher Parkes, 'Business fights hard against lawsuit initiative', *Financial Times*, 13 September 1996, p. 6. It was rejected by the voters in the 5 November 1996 election.

ings and loan ('S&L') crisis is a prominent example. With their own funds effectively insured by the US federal government, S&Ls and their depositors had every incentive to seek the highest returns independent of risk. By protecting investors from the negative effects of risk, regulation made it rational for them to incur it.

In like fashion, regulation that seeks to make equity investment 'safe' tends in fact to make it more hazardous; it provides a perverse incentive for investors to be less diligent and less vigilant. Lulled into false security by the fact that their banks or brokers are authorised, their directors are 'independent', their shares are listed, or their financial statements are audited, investors fail to exercise due diligence themselves, and make uninformed or reckless choices. As the 'expectation gap' surrounding the role of auditors reveals, investors are all too ready to believe that regulation is a guarantee of continuing soundness. But it can never be that. Nor can it ever be a substitute for careful judgement; no regulation can replace the most important prudential rule of the market: *caveat emptor*.

Other examples of regulatory moral hazard are not hard to find. Requirements for quarterly reporting can encourage 'short-termism'.[19] The US tax code has promoted bankruptcy, by encouraging both high debt and risky investments. The code favours debt, because interest payments are a deductible expense, whereas dividends are not; dividends are indeed taxed twice. When equity and dividend payouts are less important, and earnings are retained, accountability is reduced: managers have less need to seek external funds for proposed projects ... and thus less need to justify those projects.

---

19 Just as they coming under increasing attack in the US, quarterly reporting requirements are being advocated by the EU. Robert Bruce, 'Corporate Governance; the Long and the Short-term of it', *Financial Director*, 1 June 2003, p. 32.

Consider as well the official US treatment of options: the rapid increase in their use has largely been promoted by the accounting and tax codes. For accounting purposes, option grants do not have to be shown as an expense. Although a grant of shares (even shares whose sale is restricted) typically leads to a reduction in reported earnings, a grant of options does not. But perversely, options linked to performance goals do have to be set against expenses. This has dissuaded most US companies from tying options to operational targets. To make things even worse, the use of options has also been encouraged by tax legislation.[20]

Counterproductive corporate governance regulation

But isn't regulation specifically intended to improve corporate governance too straightforward to present such dangers? No, it isn't. The US Sarbanes-Oxley Act of 2002 ('SOX'), which was hastily passed in response to the Enron and WorldCom scandals, is no exception. By prohibiting auditing firms from performing a range of non-audit services for their audit clients, and requiring audit partner rotation, it may well reduce the quality both of audits and of the advice available to companies. By obliging lawyers to inform on their clients, SOX may increase illegality, as firms refrain from seeking legal advice. By requiring firms to compose their audit committees exclusively of independent directors, and

---

20 Since 1993, the direct compensation of corporate executives that can be deducted is capped at $1 million a year, unless the compensation is 'performance based'. Options have typically been structured to provide a one-way bet, further encouraging managements to engage in risky strategies. For more examples of US regulation that have had the (unintended) consequence of encouraging higher executive remuneration, see Jerry Unseem, 'CEO Pay: Have They No Shame?', *Fortune*, Vol. 147, Issue 8, pp. 56 ff..

defining independence strictly, SOX is likely to make qualified directors more difficult to locate and more expensive to appoint.[21] And by containing ill-thought through and apparently contradictory requirements, it may call all law into further disrepute. It is not surprising, therefore, that Sarbanes-Oxley has been likened to Britain's infamous Dangerous Dogs Act.[22]

The situation is, however, no better in Britain. Specifying strict conditions that must be satisfied by board candidates is as likely to diminish the availability of directors[23] in the UK as in the US. Increased legal penalties for directors have already spurred demands for reducing directors' liability[24], not least by the Higgs Report itself; similar protection is being sought by auditors[25]. And if 'widening the pool' means appointing directors without the requisite personal or professional qualities, then 'wider' will almost certainly mean 'worse'. Simply being a member of group not often found on boards does not qualify an individual for the onerous responsibilities of being a director. And coming from a group that

21 Raymond Hennessey and Janet Whitman, 'Recruiting New Board Directors Proving to Be Vexing Problem', Associated Press, 2 May 2002.

22 By, among others, Derek Higgs; Andrew Cave, 'Call for blitz on Britain's boardrooms Proposals would sweep away "cosy" corporate culture', *Daily Telegraph*, 21 January 2003, p. 29.

23 'Higgs will cause talent shortfall', *Accountancy Age*, 23 January 2003, p. 1. 'Non-exec shortfall fear', *The Times*, 22 January 2003, p. 23. [No author listed for either]

24 By, e.g., the *Financial Times* (Leader, 8 October 2002, p. 22), the Chartered Institute of Management Accountants (Charles Pretzlik, 'IoD backs British corporate governance model: boardroom review of role of non-executive directors urged not to impose further regulation on companies', *Financial Times*, 5 September 2002, p. 4), and the Institute of Chartered Accountants in England and Wales ('ICAEW'; *International Accounting Bulletin*, 27 September 2002, p. 6).

25 'Revenge of the nerds', 29 May 2003, *The Economist*, www.economist.com; no page no. cited.

is unwilling or unable to commit to the corporate objective should be an immediate disqualification.

Seeking diversity for its own sake is indeed triply misguided. It is likely to reduce the quality of directors. It presupposes the mistaken notion that representatives need to resemble their constituents in order to represent them authentically. Finally, and even more fundamentally, it ignores the fact that what the director is meant to represent is not any particular sectional constituency, but the interests of the shareholders as a whole, defined by reference to the constitutional corporate objective. Although having directors represent specific constituencies is normally associated with employee representation on Works Councils mandated by the EU[26], similar representation has been advocated for other groups: suppliers, for example, and environmental activists, and women[27]. To the extent that such groups are not shareholders, they have no legitimate claim to board representation: as the property of its shareholders, a corporation is properly accountable only to them. All the arguments against multiple accountability presented in the section on stakeholder theory apply equally against the claims of non-shareholders to board membership.

Insofar as the groups calling for special representation are themselves categories of shareholder, a different argument applies. While it is certainly appropriate for directors to be shareholders, and conversely for shareholders to be represented on the

---

26   The TUC and its Dutch and German labour union equivalents, the FNV and DGB, have also demanded that the EU provide a statutory role for employee representatives in determining executive pay packages. David Gow, 'EU unions call for boardroom pay controls', *Guardian*, 29 May 2003, p. 18.

27   Sweden has threatened legislation if at least 25 per cent of its boards are not female by the end of 2004. Chris Brown-Humes, 'Equal time in Sweden's boardrooms', *Financial Times*, 31 May 2003, p. 20.

board, the extent to which they are is a matter for the shareholders themselves to determine. Any attempt to enforce representation through regulation is necessarily counterproductive, because it reduces the ability of shareholders to run their companies as they wish.

But what about regulations to ensure that small or individual shareholders are represented on the board?[28] Don't the interests of minority shareholders deserve legislative protection? No, not so long as there are no regulatory impediments to shareholders' protecting themselves. The purpose of corporate governance is ensure that corporations pursue the corporate objectives determined by their shareholders, not to protect the interests of any one category or class of shareholder against the others. If enough of the shareholders want to, of course, they can specify that the corporation be run by and for any group they choose. But until and unless they do, directors should represent the corporation and the interests of all the shareholders, not the interests of specific shareholders.

Regulation requiring institutional investors to vote their shares[29] would also be counterproductive, however innocuous it might seem. The rationale is, presumably, that if institutional investors had to vote, they would be more likely to vote against negligent managements, and would thus better serve the interests of good corporate governance. But mandatory voting could easily lead to the opposite outcome. The 'Wall Street rule' of 'sell or

---

28 *Financial Times*, 9 December 1995, *Weekend Money*, p. 2.

29 Recommended by, e.g., Robert Monks and Allen Sykes, *Capitalism without owners will fail: A policymaker's guide to reform*, Centre for the Study of Financial Innovation, 2002, p. 31. Also recommended by the UK Labour Party (William Lewis, 'Pension funds told of duty to vote', *Financial Times*, 15 November 1995); see also Robert Taylor, 'TUC proposals round on "boardroom greed"', *Financial Times*, 25 July 1996, p. 6.

vote with management' is deeply ingrained. Requiring inertial, ill-informed institutional investors to vote might as well serve to entrench as to oust negligent incumbents; it might equally increase the reviled 'short-termism'.

'Short-termism' might also be strengthened by proposals limiting the service of directors of long standing[30] or advanced age. Regulation to enforce the opposite, however, would be at least as bad.

Consider proposals that directors be required to serve for prescribed terms of three[31], four[32] or five[33] years. Advocates contend that obliging directors to serve for fixed periods would incline them to think long term; it would also, they allege, increase company stability and directors' independence of management. Contrary to improving corporate governance, however, requiring directors to serve fixed terms is as likely to undermine it.

First, enforcing fixed terms would presumably make it more difficult for directors to resign; it would thereby frustrate an important, albeit ultimate, way of expressing disapproval of company policies. Second, if directors were required by law to serve fixed terms, they could, presumably, not be removed before their terms were over ... regardless of how negligent or incompetent they might have been. If that were so, then the effect would be

30 The Higgs Report recommends that directors serve only two terms of three years (A.7.3), and that after ten years' standing they no longer qualify as independent, regardless of their actual conduct (Para 9.14).

31 William Lewis and David Wighton, 'Labour softens on stakeholding', *Financial Times*, 26 June 1996, p. 19.

32 'Governance Revisited', leader, *Financial Times*, 22 August 1996.

33 Lipton and Rosenblum, 'A New System of Corporate Governance', *op. cit.*. See also M. Lipton, 'An end to hostile takeovers and short-termism', *Financial Times*, 27 June 1990, p. 21.

effectively to free directors from any need to be accountable to shareholders for the duration of their terms of office. Tenure might be sensible to protect the independence of Supreme Court justices, but it is neither necessary nor appropriate for company directors: they are meant to be agents of, not independent of, the shareholders. Even if directors' extended contracts could be cancelled by the company for cause, the cost of doing so would likely be prohibitive; it would certainly be more expensive than cancelling or not renewing a shorter contract. Higher costs and reduced accountability are, indeed, precisely the reasons why other critics of corporate governance want regulation to make multi-year contracts illegal .... Belief in regulation as a panacea is more common than agreement on what the regulation should require.

A third and even more dramatic effect of legislating fixed terms for directors is that it would protect them, and managements, from takeovers. If directors cannot be replaced until their extended terms expire, then even buying a company will not permit it to be controlled: regardless of how many shares may be acquired, the new owners will be unable to change the company's direction. The requirement for fixed directorial terms would both seriously thwart shareholder democracy, and insulate companies from the salutary effects of takeovers.

Whatever else may be said about this damaging consequence of fixing directorial terms, however, it certainly cannot be excused as unintended. The idea of legislating fixed terms for directors was first proposed and has since been prominently advocated by Martin Lipton, the American lawyer who is renowned for defending companies against takeover bids, and who invented the 'poison pill' ....

The effects of anti-takeover regulation are equally counterproductive. According to academic studies, state anti-takeover laws passed in the US before 1988 cost shareholders of the affected firms more than $6 billion by 1990 alone.[34] And after Pennsylvania proposed legislation limiting takeovers, companies subject to it underperformed the Standard & Poors 500 by 6.9 per cent.[35] Regulation to prevent takeovers hurts shareholders.

So does all regulation that attempts to enforce aspects of corporate governance. Because the purpose of corporate governance is to ensure that corporations respect their owners' wishes, it should always be for the shareholders to determine the degree of protection that they want, and the methods and structures that they deem best suited to achieve it. Regulation that limits shareholders' options, and reduces their freedom to control their own company as they choose, is necessarily counterproductive.

The proper role of government

Is there any role for government action? Definitely: the most valuable reforms are those which would correct existing regulation, so as to free corporate governance from government-imposed obstacles.

---

34   Jonathan M. Karpoff and Paul H. Malatesta, *Evidence on State Antitakeover Laws*, University of Washington School of Business, July/August 1990, p. 1; reported in Monks and Minnow, *PA, op. cit.*, p. 142.

35   ' ... from October 12, 1989 (the date of the first national newswire report of the bill [Act 36 of 1990]), through January 2, 1990 (when the bill was introduced in the Pennsylvania House) ... '; *ibid.*, reported in Monks and Minnow, *PA, op. cit.*, p. 120. After enactment of the law, share prices of companies which remained incorporated there fell by 4 per cent; see Stephen L. Nesbitt, *The Impact of 'Anti-Takeover' Legislation on Pennsylvania Common Stock Price*, Wilshire Associates, 27 August 1990, reported in Monks and Minnow, *PA, op. cit.*, p. 120.

In the US, for example, perverse incentives should be removed from the tax code. Unfair restrictions should be removed from securities legislation: when directors are allowed to sell their shares in response to market movements, so should other shareholders. Crucially, SEC restrictions that inhibit shareholders from nominating directors should be eliminated. Shareholders should also not be prevented by the law from proposing resolutions either about corporate elections or the 'conduct of the ordinary business of the corporation'.[36] Nor should shareholders be prevented by regulation from making proposals that are binding on the board.

Directors' duty of care and loyalty should be restored, by rejecting the 'business judgement' rule[37] and repealing state laws that limit directors' liability. Moreover, laws requiring long and staggered terms for directors should be abolished. By preventing the replacement of directors except at pre-determined intervals, such laws diminish both the board's accountability to shareholders and the reforming capabilities of takeovers.[38]

Is there anything positive that government could do to improve corporate governance? Perhaps. Improving the standards and sanctions attaching to trusteeship would help strengthen what is perhaps the weakest link in corporate governance, that between institutional investors and the ultimate owners of the assets they manage.

---

36 SEC §240.14a-8.

37 In assessing directors' compliance with fiduciary standards, the courts typically defer to the directors' business judgment unless there is clear evidence of fraud or bad faith; anyone challenging a business decision bears the burden of proof, because the business judgment rule gives directors a rebuttable presumption of correctness. See Chapter 4 above, note 30.

38 See Chapter 4 above, note 31.

Although large amounts of personal savings are in the form of private pensions[39], and most pension funds are structured as trusts, there are few mechanisms available for keeping pension fund trustees accountable. Most pensioners can neither influence the choice of the trustees governing their retirement funds, nor do anything to punish or replace them in the case of misconduct.[40] But trustees are typically subject to serious conflicts of interest. Although they have a fiduciary responsibility to protect the best interests of the beneficiaries, they are typically employees of the plan sponsor. And their advisers are firms that seek to provide services to both the plan sponsor and to the companies in which the pension fund invests. Furthermore, sponsoring companies usually know how trustees vote their shares, but the beneficiaries do not. So there is much about trusteeship that could be improved.

In conclusion, the nature of corporate governance is such that it cannot be promoted by regulation. Even if it could be, the essential rigidity of regulation, the substantial danger of unintended consequences and moral hazards, and the likelihood that regulation will harm the very groups it is intended to benefit, are fundamental reasons why regulation of corporate governance should be firmly resisted. Even rules ostensibly designed to improve accountability should not be imposed on shareholders.

What is needed to improve corporate governance is not regulation, but better understanding of, and more realistic expectations about, what corporations and business are. The best – indeed the

39 In 1999, 19.6 per cent of the UK equity market was held by company pension funds, and an additional 9.7 per cent by unit and investment trusts and pooled pension vehicles; together they represented the largest category of investor. Paul Myners, *Institutional Investment in the UK: A Review*, March 2001, Table 1.1, p. 27.

40 See pp. 96–7 above.

only – way that government can improve corporate governance is by removing existing legislative and regulatory obstacles to corporate accountability. The purpose of reforms should be to increase the power of the shareholders themselves to determine the degrees and kinds of accountability that they want to have.

The value of doing so is clear. According to a recent analysis of 1,500 stocks by the (US) National Bureau of Economic Research, companies with the most restricted shareholder rights had annual earnings and valuations between 1990 and 1999 that were almost 9 per cent lower than companies with the fewest restrictions.[41] Shareholder freedom is associated with both good corporate governance and superior corporate performance.

41 Paul Gompers, Joy Ishii and Andrew Metrick, *Corporate Governance and Equity Prices*, NBER Working Paper No. 8449, August 2001.

Section 4
Superior Solutions

8   MARKET IMPROVEMENTS

So the most commonly advocated methods for improving traditional Anglo-American corporate governance are counter-productive: the German and Japanese systems, stakeholding and regulation are more likely to undermine than to enhance genuine accountability. Contrary to popular belief, therefore, the way to secure better corporate governance is not to abandon the Anglo-American system. The challenge instead is to find better ways of implementing the Anglo-American system, so that it actually delivers in practice the advantages it promises in theory.

For corporate governance to be improved, it must provide greater assurance that corporate actions, agents and assets are directed at achieving the corporate purposes established by the corporation's shareholders. Because shareholders and their purposes are diverse, however, both the types of accountability that shareholders want, and the favoured methods of securing them, can vary significantly. The best way to reflect divergent preferences, and to discover optimum methods of fulfilling shared preferences, is to make the objectives of corporate governance clear, and to subject the mechanisms for achieving them to free competition in the marketplace.

A competitive market for corporate control

What is wanted is a 'market for corporate control'. That phrase conventionally refers to the use of takeovers to transfer corporate ownership.[1] It can, however, be used more broadly, to refer to the market in which companies compete for shareholders, and investment managers for funds, in part on the degree and kinds of accountability they afford to owners.[2] Such a competition is not wholly unknown. In the United States, individual states have long competed to be sites of company incorporation on the basis of the protection they afford to managements.[3] The need now is for comparable competition to protect the interests of owners.

The challenge is to find ways of extending the competition that already exists in respect of a company's operational performance to the corporate governance mechanisms that affect it. These include, for example, the nature of the constitutional corporate objectives, the extent to which strategic and operational matters require shareholder approval, company election procedures, the independence and quality of directors, the extent and quality of

---

1   The actual market is for securities; corporate control is a function of their ownership.

2   Such a market is recognised by the OECD: 'A market for governance arrangements should be permitted so that those arrangements that can attract investors and other resource contributors – and support competitive corporations – flourish.' OECD Business Sector Advisory Group on Corporate Governance, *Corporate Governance: Improving Competitiveness and Access to Capital in Global Markets*, Organisation for Economic Co-operation and Development, April 1988, p. 34, para. 54.

3   Lucian Arye Bebchuk and Alma Cohen, 'Firms' Decisions Where to Incorporate', Harvard Law and Economics Discussion Paper No. 351; October 2002, ECGI – Finance Working Paper No. 03/2002; available at http://papers.ssrn.com/paper.taf?abstract_id=304386.

performance-related remuneration, and the types of disclosure and audits.

Advocating a market for corporate control does not mean that corporate governance should be the sole or even the preferred criterion for assessing investments. Corporate governance is only a means; the end is always achievement of the substantive corporate objective. For business, that end is maximising shareholder value, which depends on business strategy as much as on corporate governance. In evaluating corporate governance, the focus should therefore not be on procedural 'hygiene' matters that limit corporate flexibility, or on 'box-ticking'. The aim of corporate governance is to improve the achievement of shareholders' objectives, not to interfere with corporate operations.

Studies have repeatedly suggested that shareholder value can be substantially improved by active corporate governance. The experience of the California Public Employees' Retirement System ('CalPERS')[4], one of the first and foremost of the US institutional investor activists, is instructive. The underperforming companies it has targeted for attention have routinely gone on to outperform the Standard & Poor's 500 index. According to a 1992 report[5], CalPERS's strategy (of identifying and publicising underperformance and filing shareholder proposals to bring about improvements) cost it $500,000, and generated profits of $137 million over the S&P average. That impressive result was confirmed in 1994/95:

4   The largest public pension fund in the United States, and the third largest in the world, with assets totalling $130.7 billion at 31 March 2003. CalPERS Investments, http://www.calpers.ca.gov.

5   By Wilshire Associates; reported in 'Not awakening the dead', Management Focus, *The Economist*, 10 August 1996, p. 57.

companies that trailed market averages by 66 per cent for the five years prior to CalPERS's intervenion, outperformed the S&P index by 52.5 per cent in the following five years.[6]

The value of publicising underperformers was further corroborated in 1995: 96 companies that were put on a focus list by the US Council of Institutional Investors went on to outperform the S&P 500 by 11.6 per cent in the year after they were targeted, and generated an estimated total abnormal dollar gain of $39.7 billion.[7] Furthermore, according to research published in 1996, two thirds of investors surveyed were willing to pay an average 16 per cent premium for companies that 'had good corporate governance'.[8]

The 'CalPERS Effect' was reaffirmed in 1999, the most recent year for which research is available. Shares of the 95 companies targeted by CalPERS between 1987 and 1999 trailed the Standard & Poor's 500 Index by 96 per cent in the five years before CalPERS acted, but outperformed the index by 14 per cent in the following

---

6   S .L. Nesbitt, 'Long-Term Rewards from Corporate Governance: A Study of the "CalPERS Effect" ', *Journal of Applied Corporate Finance*, Winter 1994, pp. 75–80 and 'The "CalPERS Effect": A Corporate Governance Update', 19 July 1995; quoted in CalPERS, 'Why Corporate Governance Today?: A Policy Statement', 14 August 1995, http://www.calpers.ca.gov.

7   Tim C. Opler and Jonathan Sokobin, 'Does Coordinated Institutional Activism Work? An Analysis of the Activities of the Council of Institutional Investors', October 1995; http://www.ciicentral.com/ciiabs1.htm.

8   Robert F. Felton, Alec Hudnut and Jennifer van Heeckeren, 'Putting a Value on Corporate Governance', *The McKinsey Quarterly*, 4, 1996, p. 170; see also note 41 below. It is noteworthy that when Eidos was dropped by its auditors for failing to comply with the Cadbury corporate governance guidelines, its shares immediately fell 7 per cent, despite a 20-fold increase in turnover; Jim Kelly, 'Loss of auditor hits Eidos shares', *Financial Times*, 10 August 1997, p. 16. The share price decline widened to 18.6 per cent over the following ten days; Jim Kelly, 'When auditors go on record', *Financial Times*, 21 August 1997, p. 8.

five years, adding approximately $150 million annually in additional returns to the fund.[9]

Research that denies the value of corporate governance[10] typically misidentifies corporate governance with mere 'hygiene' matters, or uses questionable surrogates for measuring shareholder activism.[11] Other challenges have failed to appreciate the free-rider problem. When even the largest institutional activists own at most 1–2 per cent of the companies they target, but their activities benefit all of a company's shares (including those owned by inactive investors), it can be hard to isolate the effects of activism.

In any case, advocating a market for corporate control is not to suggest that shareholder activism is always a good thing: it is not. Activism is sometimes ill-judged. Furthermore, the costs and constraints that apply to the active exercise of ownership rights can make activism positively counterproductive.[12] So long as the gains from improving corporate governance are slower and smaller than those obtainable from portfolio adjustment, shareholder activism is not necessarily the rational or the responsible

---

9   According to a Wilshire Associates study; reported in CalPERS, *Corporate Governance Facts*, May 2003, p. 3, www.calpers-governance.org.

10   See, for example, Charlie Weir, David Laing and Phillip J. McKnight, 'An empirical analysis of the impact of corporate governance mechanisms on the performance of UK firms', Version 2 (undated; posted 10 October 2001), http//papers.ssrn.com/paper.taf?abstract_id=ID286440; Roberta Romano, 'Less is More: Making Shareholder Activism a Valuable Mechanism of Corporate Governance', Yale Law School Program for Studies in Law, Economics, and Public Policy Working Paper # 241, Yale International Center for Finance Working Paper No. 00-10, 14 May 2000; http//papers.ssrn.com/paper.taf?abstract_id=218650.

11   Institutional ownership is no proof of shareholder activism. Nor is active corporate governance exhausted by public governance events (e.g., US proxy proposals); shareholder proposals are most likely to be resorted to at firms that are most recalcitrant and least likely to improve.

12   See Bernard S. Black, 'Shareholder Passivity Reexamined', *op. cit.*.

option. For activism to promote better corporate governance, shareholders need easier and better ways to keep their corporations on course.

Reducing the costs of shareholder activism is becoming increasingly important, however, because market trends are making activism more difficult to avoid. Generally low equity market returns and the growing concentration of ownership in institutional hands are making the sale of shares progressively less rewarding. When investment performance is measured against the market overall, selling shares of companies which constitute a large part of market capitalisation can indeed be counterproductive even for funds which are not formally indexed. The very size of US and UK institutional holdings can also make them hard to sell without depressing prices, and hard to replace with suitable alternative investments. As Georg Siemens, the founder of Deutsche Bank, pointed out more than 100 years ago, 'If one can't sell, one must care'.[13]

Moreover, voting is a legal requirement for large and increasingly important groups of international shareholders. US mutual funds, US pension funds subject to ERISA and FERSA requirements, and French pension funds[14] are all obliged to vote their shares. If UK institutional investors do not vote, they may find the companies in which they invest dominated by active overseas voters.

13 Quoted in Simon Holberton, 'A caring role for the pension funds', *Financial Times*, 13 March 1991, p. 16.

14 Article 13 of the French pension funds law of 25 March 1997 imposes 'a primary legal obligation to exercise voting rights in the interests of the beneficiaries'; attachment to June 1997 letter to delegates from R. D. Regan, Chairman, International Corporate Governance Network, Association of British Insurers, 51 Gresham Street, London EC2V 7HQ; Ref: LN32805A*INV\RREG\CORP-GOV\ PARIS.97\LETTERS.

The remainder of this chapter therefore sets out a variety of mechanisms that might be employed to make corporate governance easier and more effective: the list is not exhaustive, merely suggestive. An assortment of mechanisms is provided, because no single structure or set of structures is likely to be the best for all companies. The ends that can be pursued using the corporate form, the circumstances confronting particular corporations, the risk/reward profiles of investors, and investors' interests in and resources for exercising control over their corporations, are too diverse to be satisfied by any one model. Moreover, the very purpose of corporate governance makes any external attempt to impose corporate governance mechanisms necessarily counterproductive. The objective of corporate governance is simply to ensure that corporations are directed at achieving their shareholders' ends; it should therefore be up to the shareholders to specify what kinds of accountability they require, and how they want to achieve it. The list below is thus suggestive only.

For convenience, the discussion below refers mainly to shareholders and companies. Many of the features included are, however, ones that the beneficial owners of collective investment instruments might equally require as a condition of their investment. Conversely, the mechanisms might usefully be offered by both companies and investment managers as means of attracting funds. The mechanisms listed are intended to keep corporations more accountable to shareholders, and to keep institutional investors more accountable to the ultimate beneficiaries of the funds in their care.

Competitive mechanisms

Corporate objectives

A fundamental but often overlooked corporate governance mechanism is the corporate objective itself.[15] Companies could significantly differentiate themselves in the competition for funds by identifying their corporate objectives more precisely[16]. Specifying objectives helps to clarify both what the corporation should be achieving and what it should avoid. A corporation intended to be a business, for example, could explicitly define its sole purpose as 'maximising shareholder value by selling goods or services'. The particular kind of business might even be specified; shareholders might want to restrict a retailing corporation from becoming a manufacturer, or a manufacturer of ploughshares from switching to swords. Equally, investment trusts could specify more precisely the types of investments and strategy allowed.[17]

Whatever its objectives are, a company can make their achievement more likely by explicitly building them into its management measures and remuneration schemes. Companies could compete for shareholders by varying the extent to which their policies were genuinely performance-related, and by ensuring that the performances measured actually promoted rather than undermined the

---

15   For a useful description of the value of unitary, quantifiable objectives, see Michael C. Jensen, 'Value Maximization, Stakeholder Theory, and the Corporate Objective Function', *Journal of Applied Corporate Finance*, 14(3), autumn 2001; http://papers.ssrn.com/paper.taf?abstract_id=220671. See also John Argenti, *Your Organisation: What Is It For?*, McGraw-Hill, 1993, pp. 47, 50, 51.

16   This is not an argument against conglomerates: the purpose might be 'to maximise owner value by buying and selling other businesses'.

17   Consider the trend for 'style investing'; 'US lights the way for UK to follow', *Financial Times*, 7 June 1997, *Weekend Money*, p. 6 (no author indicated).

corporate objectives. To prevent remuneration schemes from being 'loser friendly', bonuses for executives as well as for directors could be made contingent on sustained performance, with payment deferred until the outcomes were clear.

Votes

Another competitive strategy would be to extend the scope, and reduce the costs, of voting in corporate elections. If voting were less likely to have harmful effects for shareholders, important decisions could actually depend on shareholder votes, and corporate elections could be a more effective means of improving corporate governance.

Various structural alterations might be introduced to make voting in company elections more meaningful. Each vote could refer to a single topic. Votes could be made binding rather than merely precatory. All shareholders, even those holding their shares through nominee accounts, could be entitled to receive company information and to vote. Holders of proxies could be allowed to vote on a show of hands, and to raise questions at company meetings. Shareholders could be allowed to appoint multiple corporate representatives. Managements could be prohibited from exercising the votes of shares held in treasury. Electronic means could be used to aid communication between companies and their shareholders; some or all meetings could be virtual, taking place in real time but through cyberspace.

It could be made easier for shareholders to get resolutions on to the agendas of EGMs as well as of AGMs. Companies could alter the percentage of shares required, the mandatory period of advance notice, and the extent to which shareholders were liable for distribution expenses in respect of shareholder resolutions. Companies able and willing to take advantage of modern technology could make communication with, and voting by, shareholders significantly easier and cheaper. Shareholders could also be empowered to exercise at any time (through 'written consent', once common in the US)[18] all the powers they have at general meetings.

If votes were less costly to exercise, the matters put to a shareholder vote could go far beyond the annual accounts and directors' report[19], and could serve differentially to attract investment. Votes might cover not just all increases in equity (especially important in jurisdictions where rights issues are not standard practice), but increases in debt over a stipulated limit. Shareholder approval could be made essential for all takeover or merger approaches given or received[20], and indeed for all changes affecting shareholders' rights – including, but not limited to, the introduction of poison pills and golden parachutes. Votes might also be required for all major shifts in strategy, for major operational changes, for the sale of major assets, and even for all corporate disbursements other than for specific goods or services received by the company (e.g., for contributions to political parties or charities, or arts sponsorship). Finally, shareholders might be empowered to alter[21] as well as approve reorganisation plans in bankruptcy.[22]

---

18 See Monks and Minnow, *PA*, *op.cit.*, p. 194.

19 Which UK law decrees must be presented to, but need not necessarily be approved by, the shareholders.

20 Although speed and secrecy are usually necessary to mount a successful takeover, advance shareholder approval might nonetheless be obtained for transactions of a stipulated size and nature, e.g., takeovers of domestic firms in a particular industrial sector with ROEs exceeding a target level.

21 When the law allows ....

22 Though that might have unintended consequences for creditors' willingness to lend ....

The usefulness of corporate elections could be dramatically enhanced by requiring shareholder approval for all directors' appointments and remuneration[23], and by requiring directors to stand for re-election annually. To the extent that directors were appointed for longer terms of office, those terms could be aligned rather than staggered, so that the entire board could be replaced at intervals.

Votes could be made less dangerous to exercise by disclosing their outcomes to the beneficial owners of the shares[24], while keeping them confidential from company managements. This reversal of current practice would make it easier for institutional shareholders with multiple business interests to vote against underperforming incumbents, while equipping the shares' beneficial owners to evaluate their institutional agents. Disclosure could also be made more useful if it reported the numbers of votes supporting and opposing a proposition both as a percentage of the votes cast, and of the total shares eligible to vote.[25]

Finally, corporate votes could be made more valuable, even to those who did not exercise them, if shares' voting rights

---

23 The votes prescribed by UK law in 2002 are advisory only; see Chapter 4 above, note 4. So keen are executives to avoid disclosure of their remuneration, that senior UK executives have been known to shorten their contracts on elevation to the main board. Despite management opposition, the US Association of Belltel Retirees recently won a proposal that will require shareholder approval of executive severance packages. John Wasik, 'Time to give top dogs smaller bones', *Financial Times*, 28 May 2003, p. 23.

24 Eight of the UK's top ten retail fund managers recently declared their willingness to disclose their voting positions to retail investors on request. Tony Tassell, 'Fund managers edge towards openness', *Financial Times*, 31 May 2003, p. 1. On 23 January 2003, the SEC ruled that proxy votes made by mutual funds will have to be disclosed.

25 The US SEC requires such information to be provided for votes at AGMs, typically in the next 10Q filing.

were separated from their other rights[26] and traded separately. Although ignored by many, votes are nevertheless highly valued by some[27]; if they were represented in a separate negotiable instrument, their value could be established and transferred to those who actually prized electoral power.

Directors

Companies could also compete for investors by facilitating the performance of directors' duties. For directors to fulfil their distinctive responsibilities, three general conditions must be met. Directors must be properly qualified to perform their role. They must be structurally independent of management. And they must be fully accountable to shareholders.

Identification

One notable way for companies to compete for shareholders would be to provide alternate means of selecting directors. While nomination committees of non-executive directors can serve a useful purpose, shareholders could be empowered to nominate candidates directly. Nominees could even be permitted to propose themselves: frivolous candidates could still be excluded by requiring nominations to be supported by a minimum number of shareholders, or by requiring candidates to have a minimum

---

26 Mainly economic.

27 As evidenced by the fact that Alastair Ross Goobey, then chief executive of Hermes Investment Management, was reportedly offered money to influence his vote. William Lewis, 'Fund manager was offered cash for votes', *Financial Times*, 20 September 1996, p. 9.

shareholding in the company, or by having candidates forfeit a deposit if they failed to secure a stipulated number of shareholder votes. To ensure that able candidates were not excluded from consideration, some or all of the expenses of electing directors might be for the account of the company.

Aspiring directors could be required to compete for board positions on the basis of their strategic and tactical plans for the corporation, their professional and moral judgement, their independence of and ability to direct management, and the time and expertise they could devote to protecting shareholders' interests. Because a prime way to ensure that directors serve shareholders' interests is for directors to be substantial shareholders, shareholdings of various levels might be required for all directors (and even key managers). Directors might also be required to inform shareholders of their reasons for resigning when those reasons were relevant to corporate governance or performance.

Independence

Altering the percentage of non-executive directors, and designating a lead non-executive director, and separating the roles of chief executive and chairman, are other ways in which companies could compete for investors. A company's unitary board might even be composed entirely of non-executives, with executive expertise secured for the board via executive committees. Unlike members of a German supervisory board, such a non-executive board would not represent factional interests. If its members were charged with, and remunerated on the basis of, achieving the constitutional corporate objective, they would have every incentive to refrain from non-constructive interference.

Corporations might even experiment with the extent to which their directors were allowed to be executives of any company. Shareholders might seek to employ the services of 'professional directors'[28], directors who would not be the executives of any firm, but who would be chosen specifically for their ability to safeguard shareholder interests. Even if such directors acted in a non-executive capacity for more than one firm, they might be less prone to the damaging conflicts of interest which now typically arise between executive directors and owners.

Companies could also compete for funds on the basis of the different sorts of financial and structural support they offered to directors. For directors to be able to perform their supervisory function effectively, all directors, including the non-executives, need to have full access to company information and the company's staff. Companies might, therefore, reimburse some or all of the expenses directors incurred in investigating company matters, and in taking specialist advice.

To align directors' interests with those of shareholders, substantial portions of the remuneration of both executive and non-executive directors of business corporations could be in the form of shares rather than share options or cash. The fact that all directors have equal responsibilities as directors might be emphasised by paying them all – executive and non-executive – the same directorial fees. Those directors who were also executives of the company could be paid separately for undertaking their executive

---

28   See 'Redirecting directors', Leader, *The Economist*, 17 November 1990, pp. 19–20. While both skill and integrity are obviously to be sought, the concept of 'professionalism' used here does not imply any official certification, specialist training, or accreditation by industry bodies; it is distinct from, e.g., the notion of 'chartered director' promoted by the Institute of Directors.

responsibilities. Companies could also vary the extent to which directors' (and advisers') liabilities were indemnified, contractually limited, or covered by errors and omissions insurance at company expense.

Disclosure and audits

Another significant area for competition concerns the kind of disclosures made to shareholders, above and beyond those required by law. Directors might supply interim as well as annual reports; reports might cover various sorts of risk management; financial disclosure might extend to divisional level. Companies could make the auditor's 'management letter' available to shareholders. The full cost to shareholders of pension and option plans might be made clear. When the activities of the company or its employees made insider trading a potential concern, employees might be required to clear all their securities transactions with the board or even disclose them to shareholders.

Companies could also compete on the types of auditing provided. Environmental and ethical[29] audits are increasingly being offered to supplement financial audits. Governance audits could be introduced, designed specifically to determine the extent to which a company's structures and systems, procedures and policies were actually directed at achieving the constitutional corporate objectives. Properly structured, such governance audits could enable shareholders to evaluate the performance of directors, and enable directors to assess the conduct of other stakeholders.

---

29 For the description of a realistic ethical audit, see Sternberg, *JB, op. cit.*, pp. 240–3.

Enforcement

Companies could also compete on the enforcement methods used to ensure the satisfactoriness of their governance and of their performance. A governance committee[30] could be charged with ensuring strict adherence to the corporate purpose.[31] Theoretically, of course, this is the job of the board overall. To the extent that a board is subject to significant conflicts of interest, however, specific oversight of the corporate purposes might be prudent.

The governance committee could supplement or supplant the traditional audit committee. All auditors, internal and external, financial and other, could usefully be appointed by, and report to, the governance committee. In addition, the governance committee could ensure that the corporation's management accounts provided managers with the information they needed for achieving the corporate purposes, and that reports to shareholders provided the information necessary for assessing corporate performance. Finally, the governance committee could also serve as a conduit for concerns about the conduct of the corporation, including those of shareholders and those disclosed through the company's critical information systems.

---

30 Typically consisting exclusively of non-executive directors; this concept of the governance committee was discussed in Sternberg, *JB*, *op. cit.*. For a variation on the theme, the Policy Auditing Committee, see, Robert A. G. Monks, 'Fund Managers: To Whom Are They Accountable?', presentation at *Economist* Conference, London, 5 December 1991; http://www.lens-inc.com/info/econo.htm.

31 In Japan, the Audit Committee is charged with the board's monitoring function including evaluating the extent to which corporate objectives are met. *JJTI*, *op. cit.*.

Critical information systems

Critical information is information that is vital for a company's proper functioning. As such, it can consist of information that is critical of a company's functioning. For a company to improve its performance or its governance, it must know in what ways its current activities fall short of its aims. Much of the damaging and counterproductive conduct of corporations occurs because people with critical information lack power, while those with power lack essential information.

Critical information systems[32] should ensure that managers and directors and owners are routinely confronted with, not shielded from, uncomfortable facts. Companies could therefore compete on the extent to which they made it more rewarding[33] to identify and resolve problems than to ignore them[34], and on the basis to which they used their stakeholders, particularly their employees and their customers, as a natural early-warning system.

Institutional investors

Institutional investors that are corporate in form have access to all the mechanisms listed above. When institutional investors are constituted as trusts, however, other mechanisms may be

---

32 For a description of the function, operation and structuring of critical information systems, see Sternberg, *JB*, *op. cit.*, pp. 208–15, 224–6.

33 A traditional obstacle to employees' suggesting improvements has been the lack of identification between the interests of employees and those of the owners: if productivity gains mean staff cuts, employees have a clear incentive not to recommend them. The answer lies in a strict observance of distributive justice, which rewards vigilance in service of the corporate goal, and in properly structured performance-related remuneration, which gives everyone an interest in pursuing the corporate goal ethically.

34 Though it should be recognised that it is better still for problems not to arise.

necessary. Trust deeds could specify more precisely both the trust objectives and the ways of handling trust assets.[35] They might require trustees to disclose more information and to report more frequently to the beneficiaries and/or the donors. Trust deeds could also make it easier to challenge the conduct of trustees by explicitly indicating criteria of mismanagement, or by reimbursing the expenses of those who successfully challenged trustees' conduct. With so much of the nation's wealth held in the form of pension funds and other trusts, it is important that mechanisms be devised to align the interests of trustees with those of the beneficiaries whose interests they are meant to protect.

Metamechanisms

It may be protested that a proliferation of mechanisms will make investing more complex, without making corporate governance any more effective. And it is true that some investors may be as incapable of identifying and evaluating corporate governance mechanisms as they are of assessing corporate performance. Once again, however, the market can fill the gap.

Just as commercial organisations now provide information about creditworthiness, and about the extent to which companies meet so-called 'ethical investment' criteria, they could equally well provide data on the kinds and efficacy of the corporate governance mechanisms offered by particular companies.[36] Some screening is

35 Had trust deeds been drawn up more carefully, much of the controversy surrounding the disposition of pension fund surpluses might have been avoided.

36 Such organisations already exist, e.g., the US Institutional Shareholder Services ('ISS') and The Corporate Monitoring Project. Governance ratings services are also provided by, e.g., Standard & Poor's, GovernanceMetrics and The Corporate Library. The UK National Association of Pension Funds has long provided

already provided by institutional investor interest groups and stock exchanges; to the extent that exchanges represented competing commercial markets rather than national champions, that service might well be extended. Furthermore, as corporate governance comes to be recognised as a factor in investment decisions, it is likely to attract the attention of investment analysts.

Investors might also take advantage of 'professional owners'. Some public companies[37] specialise in investing in other corporations, and take an active interest in the ways those companies are run. A similar function is increasingly performed by private buyout specialists[38] in respect of the businesses they finance, and by specialist corporate governance funds.[39] In their different ways, such 'professional owners' all have the resources and expertise to do more than just understand and monitor a securities portfolio; they can actively contribute to the direction and even the management of the businesses in which they invest. By commanding top performance from those companies, such professional owners serve their own interests, and render a significant service to those who invest along with them.[40]

---

guidance on corporate governance matters, and in May 2003 formed a joint venture with ISS; the venture, Research, Recommendations and Electronic Voting, will provide information on more than 22,000 companies in 80 markets. Florian Gimbel, 'US investors to take more activist role in UK', *Financial Times*, 26 May 2003, p. 2.

37 E.g., Berkshire Hathaway in the US; historically, Hanson Industries in the UK and Dynaction in France performed a similar role.

38 Such as the US Kohlberg Kravis Roberts.

39 E.g., Hermes in the UK, and the Lens Fund in the US from 1992–2000.

40 Even their performance must be monitored, however: consider the successful shareholder battle with Hanson to retain full rights to nominate directors and amend corporate resolutions. Norma Cohen, 'Hanson backs down over proposed rule changes', *Financial Times*, 18 June 1993, p. 17.

Whatever mechanisms are used, however, the importance of good corporate governance is being recognised by investors. According to an April/May 2002 survey of 201 institutional investors in 31 countries, representing institutions with $9 trillion of assets under management, corporate governance is at least as important as financial performance in influencing their investment decisions; 63 per cent of the investors surveyed would avoid companies altogether on the basis of their corporate governance practices, and approximately 77 per cent would pay premiums of between 11 per cent and 41 per cent for good corporate governance.[41]

The good corporate governance that is valued by investors is also properly their responsibility. And that is because corporate governance is just about keeping corporations directed at the ends chosen by the shareholders. Shareholders must be clear about what they want from the companies that they own, and must exert the effort necessary to keep directors accountable for achieving those goals. That requires increasing, not decreasing, accountability to shareholders.

The way to respond to flaws in current Anglo-American practice is therefore not to imitate Germany or Japan, or to enshrine stakeholder theory, or to increase the regulation of corporate activities. The way to improve Anglo-American corporate govern-

---

41 Paul Coombes, and Mark Watson, *Global Investor Opinion Survey 2002*, McKinsey & Co., July 2002, www.mckinsey.com/corporate governance. According to a previous survey of 374 institutional investors in the US, UK, France and Australia holding approximately 65 per cent of the world's $23,400 billion shareholdings, 71 per cent had 'pulled back' from investing in companies because of their poor corporate governance. *Furthering the Global Dialogue on Corporate Governance: 1998 International Survey of Institutional Investors*, Russell Reynolds Associates; reported in Jane Martinson, 'Call for governance standards', *Financial Times*, 6 April 1998, p. 10. The decline may be the result of improvements in general levels of corporate governance.

ance is instead to bring practice into line with theory, by freeing shareholders from regulatory obstacles, and allowing them to choose how best to hold their corporations to account.

REFERENCES

Works cited in more than one chapter

Cadbury Committee (1992), *Report on the Financial Aspects of Corporate Governance*, London: Gee Publishing.

Charkham, Jonathan (1995), *Keeping Good Company: A Study of Corporate Governance in Five Countries*, Oxford: Oxford University Press.

The Economist

EU Green Paper (2001), *Promoting a European framework for corporate social responsibility*, European Commission Directorate-General for Employment and Social Affairs, Unit EMPL/D.1, July; 'EUcsr'.

Financial Times

Greenbury Committee (1998), *Directors' Remuneration: Report of the Study Group Chaired by Sir Richard Greenbury*, London: Gee Publishing, 17 July.

Hampel Committee on Corporate Governance (1998), *Final Report*, London: Gee Publishing, January.

Higgs, Derek (2003), *Review of the role and effectiveness of non-executive directors*, London: Department of Trade and Industry, January.

Kochan, Nicholas and Michael Syrett (1991), *New Directions in Corporate Governance*, Business International Limited.

Monks, Robert A. G. and Nell Minnow (1991), *Power and Account-ability* ('*PA*'), New York: HarperCollins.

—— (2001), *Corporate Governance* ('*CG*'), 2nd edn, Oxford: Black-well.

Social Sciences Research Network, www.ssrn.com

Sternberg, Elaine (2000), *Just Business: Business Ethics in Action*, 2nd edn, Oxford: Oxford University Press; 1st edn, Little, Brown 1994.

Tricker, Robert I. (1994), *International Corporate Governance: Text, Readings and Cases*, Englewood Cliffs, NJ: Prentice Hall.

ABOUT THE IEA

The Institute is a research and educational charity (No. CC 235 351), limited by guarantee. Its mission is to improve understanding of the fundamental institutions of a free society with particular reference to the role of markets in solving economic and social problems.

The IEA achieves its mission by:

- a high-quality publishing programme
- conferences, seminars, lectures and other events
- outreach to school and college students
- brokering media introductions and appearances

The IEA, which was established in 1955 by the late Sir Antony Fisher, is an educational charity, not a political organisation. It is independent of any political party or group and does not carry on activities intended to affect support for any political party or candidate in any election or referendum, or at any other time. It is financed by sales of publications, conference fees and voluntary donations.

In addition to its main series of publications the IEA also publishes a quarterly journal, *Economic Affairs*, and has two specialist programmes – Environment and Technology, and Education.

The IEA is aided in its work by a distinguished international Academic Advisory Council and an eminent panel of Honorary Fellows. Together with other academics, they review prospective IEA publications, their comments being passed on anonymously to authors. All IEA papers are therefore subject to the same rigorous independent refereeing process as used by leading academic journals.

IEA publications enjoy widespread classroom use and course adoptions in schools and universities. They are also sold throughout the world and often translated/reprinted.

Since 1974 the IEA has helped to create a world-wide network of 100 similar institutions in over 70 countries. They are all independent but share the IEA's mission.

Views expressed in the IEA's publications are those of the authors, not those of the Institute (which has no corporate view), its Managing Trustees, Academic Advisory Council members or senior staff.

Members of the Institute's Academic Advisory Council, Honorary Fellows, Trustees and Staff are listed on the following page.

The Institute gratefully acknowledges financial support for its publications programme and other work from a generous benefaction by the late Alec and Beryl Warren.

Other papers recently published by the IEA include:

WHO, What and Why?

Transnational Government, Legitimacy and the World Health Organization
Roger Scruton
Occasional Paper 113; ISBN 0 255 36487 3
£8.00

The World Turned Rightside Up

A New Trading Agenda for the Age of Globalisation
John C. Hulsman
Occasional Paper 114; ISBN 0 255 36495 4
£8.00

The Representation of Business in English Literature

Introduced and edited by Arthur Pollard
Readings 53; ISBN 0 255 36491 1
£12.00

Anti-Liberalism 2000

The Rise of New Millennium Collectivism
David Henderson
Occasional Paper 115; ISBN 0 255 36497 0
£7.50

Capitalism, Morality and Markets

Brian Griffiths, Robert A. Sirico, Norman Barry & Frank Field
Readings 54; ISBN 0 255 36496 2
£7.50

A Conversation with Harris and Seldon

Ralph Harris & Arthur Seldon
Occasional Paper 116; ISBN 0 255 36498 9
£7.50

Malaria and the DDT Story

Richard Tren & Roger Bate
Occasional Paper 117; ISBN 0 255 36499 7
£10.00

A Plea to Economists Who Favour Liberty: Assist the Everyman

Daniel B. Klein
Occasional Paper 118; ISBN 0 255 36501 2
£10.00

Waging the War of Ideas

John Blundell
Occasional Paper 119; ISBN 0 255 36500 4
£10.00

The Changing Fortunes of Economic Liberalism

Yesterday, Today and Tomorrow
David Henderson
Occasional Paper 105 (new edition); ISBN 0 255 36520 9
£12.50

The Global Education Industry

Lessons from Private Education in Developing Countries
James Tooley
Hobart Paper 141 (new edition); ISBN 0 255 36503 9
£12.50

Saving Our Streams

*The Role of the Anglers' Conservation Association in
Protecting English and Welsh Rivers*
Roger Bate
Research Monograph 53; ISBN 0 255 36494 6
£10.00

Better Off Out?

The Benefits or Costs of EU Membership
Brian Hindley & Martin Howe
Occasional Paper 99 (new edition); ISBN 0 255 36502 0
£10.00

The Road to Serfdom

The Reader's Digest *condensed version*
Friedrich A. Hayek
Occasional Paper 122; ISBN 0 255 36530 6
£7.50

Bastiat's *The Law*

Introduction by Norman Barry
Occasional Paper 123; ISBN 0 255 36509 8
£7.50

A Globalist Manifesto for Public Policy

Charles Calomiris
Occasional Paper 124; ISBN 0 255 36525 X
£7.50

Euthanasia for Death Duties

Putting Inheritance Tax Out of Its Misery
Barry Bracewell-Milnes
Research Monograph 54; ISBN 0 255 36513 6
£10.00

Liberating the Land

The Case for Private Land-use Planning

Mark Pennington

Hobart Paper 143; ISBN 0 255 36508 x

£10.00

IEA Yearbook of Government Performance 2002/ 2003

Edited by Peter Warburton

Yearbook 1; ISBN 0 255 36532 2

£15.00

Britain's Relative Economic Performance, 1870– 1999

Nicholas Crafts

Research Monograph 55; ISBN 0 255 36524 1

£10.00

Should We Have Faith in Central Banks?

Otmar Issing

Occasional Paper 125; ISBN 0 255 36528 4

£7.50

The Dilemma of Democracy
Arthur Seldon
Hobart Paper 136 (reissue); ISBN 0 255 36536 5
£10.00

Capital Controls: a 'Cure' Worse Than the Problem?
Forrest Capie
Research Monograph 56; ISBN 0 255 36506 3
£10.00

The Poverty of 'Development Economics'
Deepak Lal
Hobart Paper 144 (reissue); ISBN 0 255 36519 5
£15.00

Should Britain Join the Euro?
The Chancellor's Five Tests Examined
Patrick Minford
Occasional Paper 126; ISBN 0 255 36527 6
£7.50

Post-Communist Transition: Some Lessons
Leszek Balcerowicz
Occasional Paper 127; ISBN 0 255 36533 0
£7.50

A Tribute to Peter Bauer

John Blundell et al.

Occasional Paper 128; ISBN 0 255 36531 4

£10.00

Employment Tribunals

Their Growth and the Case for Radical Reform

J. R. Shackleton

Hobart Paper 145; ISBN 0 255 36515 2

£10.00

Fifty Economic Fallacies Exposed

Geoffrey E. Wood

Occasional Paper 129; ISBN 0 255 36518 7

£12.50

A Market in Airport Slots

Keith Boyfield (editor), David Starkie, Tom Bass & Barry Humphreys

Readings 56; ISBN 0 255 36505 5

£10.00

Money, Inflation and the Constitutional Position of the Central Bank

Milton Friedman & Charles A. E. Goodhart

Readings 57; ISBN 0 255 36538 1

£10.00

railway.com

Parallels between the early British railways and the ICT revolution
Robert C. B. Miller
Research Monograph 57; ISBN 0 255 36534 9
£12.50

The Regulation of Financial Markets

Edited by Philip Booth & David Currie
Readings 58; ISBN 0 255 36551 9
£12.50

Climate Alarmism Reconsidered

Robert L. Bradley Jr
Hobart Paper 146; ISBN 0 255 36541 1
£12.50

Government Failure: E. G. West on Education

Edited by James Tooley & James Stanfield
Occasional Paper 130; ISBN 0 255 36552 7
£12.50

Waging the War of Ideas

John Blundell
Second edition
Occasional Paper 131; ISBN 0 255 36547 0
£12.50